821.7
(WOR)

4678

D1492001

cirencester
college
a beacon college

Literature in Perspective

General Editor: Kenneth H. Grose

Wordsworth

Literature in Perspective

Wordsworth

Margaret Drabble

Evans Brothers Limited, London

Published by Evans Brothers Limited

Montague House, Russell Square, London W.C.1

© Margaret Drabble 1966

First published 1966

Reprinted 1968

Set in 11 on 12 point Fournier and printed in Great Britain by

C. Tinling & Co. Ltd., Liverpool, London and Prescot

237 44385 6 cased   PR 4935

237 44405 4 limp

Literature in Perspective

Of recent years, the ordinary man who reads for pleasure has been gradually excluded from that great debate in which every intelligent reader of the classics takes part. There are two reasons for this: first, so much criticism floods from the world's presses that no one but a scholar living entirely among books can hope to read it all; and second, the critics and analysts, mostly academics, use a language that only their fellows in the same discipline can understand.

Consequently criticism, which should be as 'inevitable as breathing'—an activity for which we are all qualified—has become the private field of a few warring factions who shout their unintelligible battle cries to each other but make little communication to the common man.

Literature in Perspective aims at giving a straightforward account of literature and of writers—straightforward both in content and in language. Critical jargon is as far as possible avoided; any terms that must be used are explained simply; and the constant preoccupation of the authors of the Series is to be lucid.

It is our hope that each book will be easily understood, that it will adequately describe its subject without pretentiousness, so that the intelligent reader who wants to know about Donne or Keats or Shakespeare will find enough in it to bring him up to date on critical estimates.

Even those who are well read, we believe, can benefit from a lucid exposition of what they may have taken for granted, and perhaps—dare it be said?—not fully understood.

K. H. G.

Contents

The Author

Margaret Drabble, B.A., is a novelist and the author of *A Summer Birdcage*, *The Garrick Year*, *The Millstone* and *Jerusalem the Golden*.

Acknowledgements

The two portraits of William Wordsworth by B. R. Haydon and that by Sir Francis Legatt Chantrey are reproduced by permission of the Trustees of the National Portrait Gallery. The engraving 'Rydal Water and Grasmere' is reproduced by permission of the *Radio Times* Hulton Picture Library, and the photograph 'Springtime at Rydal Water' by permission of G. P. Abraham Ltd., Keswick.

Wordsworth

Very few people enjoy everything that Wordsworth wrote. His output was large, and more than usually varied and uneven in quality. His works have of course been written about and discussed from very many different angles, but nevertheless I think there is still a tendency, despite recent criticism, to think of him purely and simply as a nature poet, with all the peculiar strengths and weaknesses that this implies. Certainly I thought of him as a nature poet until I got down to reading his poetry for myself, and so the shock I had when I found that he was so much more than this was one of those rare and exciting shocks of discovery; my first readings of *The Idiot Boy* and *The Prelude*, for instance, were full of amazed surprise and admiration. So I must confess to a slight personal bias towards these earlier works, which I think, all in all, have received less than their fair share of attention. I may also seem to have spent an unduly large amount of space in describing the poetical background to Wordsworth's works, but this is deliberate and I think necessary: very few people who are not close students of the whole course of English Literature realize what a great original and revolutionary Wordsworth in fact was, and there is really not much point in reading the *Lyrical Ballads* and the *Preface* without some notion of the extreme novelty of Wordsworth's position. His true greatness is seen best in contrast with the poetic barrenness out of which he suddenly, amazingly appeared.

References in the text to Wordsworth's works are taken throughout from the five volume edition, *The Poetical Works by*

William Wordsworth, by E. de Selincourt and Helen Darbishire, published by the Oxford University Press; references from *The Prelude* are from the 1805 version, edited by de Selincourt, and printed separately by the O.U.P.

M. D.

I

Wordsworth the Man

Of all the great English poets, Wordsworth has surely been one of the most disliked, mocked, parodied, derided and misunderstood. Ever since his first poems were published, nearly two centuries ago, he has been accused of all kinds of literary crimes, the worst of which is perhaps dullness. To people who do not know or do not like his poetry, he presents an image made up of all kinds of forbidding and unpleasant characteristics: he is a pious, grey-haired, elderly Victorian grandfather; a puritanical, humourless water-drinker; a lover of Nature, friend to butterflies, bees and little daisies; in fact a sentimental tedious old bore, with a moral reflection ready for any subject that should come up, from Alpine scenery to railways or his neighbour's spade. I need hardly say that this image could not be further from the important truth about Wordsworth, but on the other hand there is no point in denying that there is some truth in it. Wordsworth became a pious and respectable old man, but he did not begin that way. His later writings and life have unfortunately managed to cast a huge backward shadow over all his early work and intentions, so that it is very hard for us today to see his great poems without the prejudice that his later work caused.

Wordsworth, as a poet and as a man, was full of mystery and contradictions. Perhaps the greatest and most confusing mystery of all is the fact that at a certain point in his life he ceased to be a great poet, and became a quite mediocre one, and at times a positively appalling one. All critics seem to agree about this; all of them admit that at some point in his life he started to decline as a poet, though they argue about the actual date at which he lost his power. Some say 1815, some 1810, and one or two are bold enough to say that he wrote hardly anything that was worth writing after 1805, when he was himself thirty-five. As he lived to be eighty, it is plain that he had rather a long time in which to write inferior poetry, and he managed to produce a vast amount. It is not of course thoroughly bad; there are enough fine lines and phrases scattered through his very last poems to console his addicts, and some of his admirers are loyal to him to the bitter end. It is also true that the more one reads and studies any poet or writer, the more one comes to like him, and the more excuses one is prepared to make for his weakness and oddities, just as one is more prepared to excuse the weaknesses of a relative than those of a total stranger. This is perhaps one of the reasons why critics are kinder to Wordsworth than the ordinary reader; they have to be on their guard against over-indulgence. An ordinary reader, picking up Wordsworth's Collected Works and opening it at random, is just as likely to hit upon something thoroughly tedious and undistinguished as he is to hit upon a good poem, and it might quite reasonably put him off for life. If in need of a reminder of the depths to which Wordsworth can sink, one has only to look at a piece like *On the Power of Sound*, which Wordsworth wrote when he was in his late fifties. It is as meaningless, overblown and worthless a piece as any great poet ever produced, and full of the very faults that he attacked so violently when he was a young man; it is almost unbelievable that a poet who could write so badly could also write well. The most devoted Wordsworthian could hardly read it without a shudder.

What, then, happened to Wordsworth? What is the explanation of the extraordinary inequality of his poetry? These questions have often been asked, and there is no one satisfactory answer. The explanation must lie somewhere in his own life story, and in the conflicts and tragedies he went through before acquiring the somewhat selfish tranquillity of his old age. In a later chapter an effort will be made to suggest a few reasons for the changes that came over him; all I want to do at this point is to make clear that when we think of Wordsworth, today, we think not only of the original, daring and energetic poet he was in his youth, but also of the elderly man who wrote Odes of public thanksgiving about Waterloo, sonnets on the wickedness of bringing railways into the Lake District, and dreary blank verse reflections about parsons in country churchyards. The second image has clouded and obscured the first: we look at him from the wrong end of time. We are under his influence still, for bad as well as for good, and we have to make an effort to forget the old man before we can look straight at the young one.

It is harder to imagine anyone further from the pious conformist conservative sage than the young Wordsworth. He was in every sense a rebel and a revolutionary. In politics, in literature, in his emotional life he reacted against the conventions of his age; he made his own way. When much of England was shrinking back from the very idea of the French Revolution in alarm and dismay, Wordsworth was himself in France, seeing things with his own eyes; the zeal and hopes of the downtrodden people warmed his imagination, and inspired some of his finest poetry. So unorthodox were his political views that a few years later, when he and Coleridge were leading a quiet life in the West Country, the Home Office actually sent spies after them to see if they were hatching revolutionary plots against the peace of England. In his sexual life, too, he did not abide by the strict and narrow moral codes that came into force during his own lifetime; while in France he fell in love with a woman a few years older than himself, and became at the age of twenty-two the father of a daughter, Caroline. He never married his first love, Annette, and the scandal of her existence was so effectively concealed by his Victorian admirers, relatives and biographers that the main facts of this love affair were completely hidden for many years, and did not come to light again until this century. This story is a fascinating example of the effect that the elderly man's reputation had on the young man's; the young and passionate man that Wordsworth was in his prime became so obscured and swallowed up by the dutiful husband, father and grandfather that the very evidence of his former nature was lost. A mistress and an illegitimate daughter cannot, however, be argued away; they existed, and at the time everyone knew that they existed. William and his sister Dorothy discuss the Annette problem quite openly in their letters; whatever anxieties Annette and Caroline caused him, they were not anxieties about his own social respectability. It was only later that they got shuffled out of the way, in respect for an ever-narrowing code of conduct.

The young Wordsworth was an individualist in religion, just as he was in politics and passion. He was never an atheist and never anti-Christian, but he had little respect for established religion or conventional piety; the thought of becoming a clergyman filled him with horror, and he writes with a disrespectful gloom of the prospect of 'vegetating on a paltry curacy'. His family wanted him to go into the church, for it was the safest and most respectable profession open to a young man like himself, with education and no money, but he was determinded to resist their persuasions; he did not want to be a clergyman, he wanted to write, and he preferred the thought of writing poetry to the lure of a safe and regular income. The older Wordsworth might well have chosen differently, and certainly would not have regarded the clergy with disrespect, for in later life Wordsworth became a regular churchgoer, much given to writing dutiful pieces in order to raise church funds, and to lengthy praise of the Anglican Church. He even produced a long sequence of Ecclesiastical Sonnets, on the history of Christianity in Britain, most of which are very ordinary. As in the other parts of his life, the habits of the older man conceal the faith of the younger; the religious and mystical experiences of Wordsworth as a young man have nothing whatever to do with organized Christianity. Nor do they have very much to do with other, less orthodox doctrines that are said to have influenced him. Although it is possible to see in his work reflections from the ideas of certain eighteenth-century thinkers, such as David Hartley and Rousseau, Wordsworth was no more a systematic believer in their philosophies than he was an orthodox Christian; as a young man he trusted far more to the evidence of his own experiences than to doctrines and theories. He was more affected by people he knew than by books he read.

Bearing in mind the marked difference between the two halves of Wordsworth's life, it might be useful to look at a brief outline of the principal events of his career; the dividing line between the young man and the old is not very clearly revealed in a straightforward biography, but will be seen more fully in the more detailed discussion of the poetry itself.

A BRIEF BIOGRAPHY

Wordsworth was born at Cockermouth, Cumberland, in 1770. He had an elder brother, two younger brothers, and an only sister, Dorothy. He had a happy, healthy, unrestricted childhood, though this was marred by the death of both his parents; his mother died when he was eight, his father when he was fourteen. His father had been agent to Lord Lowther, and his early death had serious consequences for his children; he left his financial affairs in a mess, and his children had to conduct a lengthy battle against Lord Lowther to regain the money they should have inherited. His death also split the family; William was left largely to the care of his maternal grandparents at Penrith, who apparently did not like him very much. Certainly he found them strict and oppressive. His sister Dorothy, of whom he was very fond, was sent away to another branch of the family, and for many years he hardly saw her.

However, despite these misfortunes, William seems to have had a fairly happy childhood. He went away when he was nine to Grammar School at Hawkshead, where he did well; he was passionately attached to the countryside round Hawkshead, and remembered it many years afterwards with gratitude and love. In 1787 he went up to Cambridge, where he led a social rather than a studious life; he had no ambition to do well in examinations, and read to please himself rather than to please his examiners. When he obtained his degree in 1791, he did not know what to do with himself, having little money and no leaning to any particular career, so he went abroad to France for several months. While in France, under the influence of a French officer called Beaupuis, his political sympathies were aroused by the social injustice that he saw there, and he became attached to the cause of the French Revolution. He also fell in love with a French woman, Annette Vallon, who bore him a daughter, Caroline, in December 1792.

He himself returned to England before his daughter was born. The next few years of his life were very unsettled, and full of unhappy wanderings. He had already started to write poetry, and had thoughts of a literary career, but when his first poems were published (*Evening Walk, Descriptive Sketches*) in 1793, they were poorly received. He was also suffering from anxiety about Annette, and about the violent course of events in France; his mental outlook was thoroughly confused. It was at this stage in his life that he is said to have been impressed by the ideas of Godwin, the philosopher, whom he may well have met through his first publisher, Joseph Johnson, who befriended many of the radical authors of London. Godwin's ideas, which are both radical and anarchic, have been traced in early poems like *Guilt and Sorrow* (1794) and in Wordsworth's only poetic drama, *The Borderers* (1795–6). Godwin believed that criminals are the victims of society, not offenders against society, and that (to put it crudely) the convict is less guilty than the king. These ideas are commonly supposed to have increased the moral confusion of Wordsworth's attitude to the French Revolution, and it is true that Wordsworth shared certain of Godwin's attitudes (such as dislike of monarchy), but nevertheless his democracy owes more to Beaupuis, and his confusion to his personal troubles, than either owe to Godwin's *Political Justice*.

In 1796, helped by an unexpected legacy from a friend, Raisley Calvert, whom he had attended in his last illness, Wordsworth set up house with his sister Dorothy at Racedown in Dorset; they helped out their finances by caring for the motherless child of a friend. This was the beginning of a new period in his life. Dorothy had always dreamed of keeping house for William, and with her constant love and care he seems to have found a new peace and happiness. It was in 1795 that he met the person who, next to Dorothy, was to have the most profound influence upon him—Samuel Taylor Coleridge, the poet, lecturer, and Unitarian preacher. The details of their first meeting are lost, but Coleridge had admired Wordsworth's poems before knowing him, and their admiration quickly became mutual. In 1797 William and Dorothy moved to Alfoxden, to be near Coleridge who was living with his wife at Nether Stowey. Wordsworth and Coleridge had a highly stimulating effect upon each other; their views on literature and politics were similar without being identical, and together they conceived the idea of the *Lyrical Ballads*, a collection of poems which they published jointly and anonymously in two editions, in 1798 and 1800, by a Bristol publisher.

The story of their collaboration is told at length in Coleridge's *Biographia Literaria* (1817): Coleridge says that the original idea was for an equal quantity of poems from each author, with his own 'endeavours directed towards persons and characters supernatural or at least romantic', while Wordsworth was 'to give the charm of novelty to things of everyday' (Chapter 14). However, as he admits, Wordsworth was so much more productive and industrious that the vast majority of the *Lyrical Ballads* are by him alone; Coleridge's only major and outstanding contribution was his supernatural tale, *The Ancient Mariner*.

After a brief visit to Germany with Dorothy in 1799, Wordsworth removed to Grasmere in the Lake District. They were to live permanently in the Lake District from this time on, though they moved from their small cottage to Allan Bank in 1808, and again to Rydal Mount in 1813. In 1802 William and Dorothy visited France, where they saw Annette and Caroline; on their return William married his childhood friend, Mary Hutchinson. They were to have five children, two of whom died in infancy.

The years at Grasmere were the most productive of

Wordsworth's life, and it was there that he wrote all his best poetry. From this time onwards his life was settled, secure and outwardly uneventful. He became recognized as a major poet; his financial affairs were eased by the payment of the Lowther debt, by the kindness of a wealthy patron, Sir George Beaumont, by the sale of his poems, and by his appointment in 1813 as Stamp Distributor for Westmorland. Gradually, his political views began to change, as his way of life had changed, and he came to look back on his early revolutionary sympathies with regret. He continued to write a great deal, but the quality of his poetry began to deteriorate as early as 1805.

His longest work, *The Excursion* (originally intended as part of an even longer and more ambitious work), appeared in 1814; it was strongly influenced by Coleridge's faith that Wordsworth should try to write a 'philosophic poem'. Much of his remaining poetry shows in its subject matter the failure of his inspiration; there are historical and classical poems, and many poems written on and about his various tours of the Continent and Scotland (1820, 1828, 1831, 1833, 1836). Subjects taken from nearer home had ceased to interest him. But his life, though apparently tranquil enough, was not without its tragedies: the loss of his brother John in 1805, the early death of two children, the illness of Dorothy (who began to fail in 1829, and never recovered, though she outlived her brother), his continual estrangements from the unhappy, difficult Coleridge, and finally the unwelcome marriage and death of his daughter Dora, all helped to cloud his later years. In 1843, at the age of seventy-three, he became Poet Laureate, somewhat against his will, and he died in 1850.

During his lifetime he was acquainted with many of the eminent literary figures of his day. He knew Lamb, Southey, Hazlitt, de Quincey, Godwin. His house was always overflowing with guests, and towards the end of his life it became a place of pilgrimage for total strangers. In some ways his life seems to be a highly successful model literary career, crowned with every distinction; his domestic life, too, has all the marks of peace and happiness. Yet under the surface there were always

18

strange and troubling powers at work; he never settled down with entire complacency into the role of grand old man of Literature. As one of the closest friends of his later years said, in a remark that has the ring of truth, 'His was a strong, but not a happy old age'.

2

Wordsworth's Literary Background

In the account of Wordsworth's life, I have tried to show how very far Wordsworth was as a young man from the conventional figure of his later years. In politics, in religion, and in his emotional life he was unorthodox and original. But it is in his literary views that his originality is most powerful and most important. There were plenty of other radicals and anarchists in England, but on the subject of poetry Wordsworth (with the backing of Coleridge) stood alone. In this field he was a lone pioneer. The date of the publication of the *Lyrical Ballads* (1798) is one of the most important single dates in the history of English Literature, for it marks the end of an age, and the beginning of a new one. When the first edition of the *Lyrical Ballads* came out, Wordsworth was twenty-eight; it was thirty-nine years before Victoria came to the throne, a fact which should be remembered by those who think of Wordsworth as a Victorian poet. The poems in this one small volume were a revolution in poetry; they were completely new, and like all new things they came in for a good deal of ridicule, misunderstanding, and devoted admiration. It is always dangerous to assert that any literary achievement is entirely original, because it must always be linked, however obscurely, to what has gone before, but nevertheless as far as anything in literature is ever new, the *Lyrical Ballads* were, and Wordsworth knew that they were. Their originality poses some problems.

1. The first question to ask is, perhaps, why were they so different, and what were they so different from?

2. Granted that they were different, did Wordsworth intend them to be so, and for what reasons?

3. And, finally, are they merely different, or are they also good? (On this last point, one might as well note here as anywhere that it is perfectly possible for something to be new, important, good in intention and in effect, without being in itself successful. The *Lyrical Ballads* might well be, as some have thought, a good influence, without being in themselves good poetry; there are many works, now unreadable, such as Sylvester's translation of a French epic by Du Bartas, which in their time had a profound effect on the course of literature. This work, published in 1605, cannot now be read with pleasure, but its effect upon Milton was profound, and without it *Paradise Lost* would have been a different poem.)

The *Lyrical Ballads* were, quite simply, different from anything that any English poet had published before 1798. They were different in language, in intention, and in subject matter. In order to make this statement mean anything, it is necessary to look briefly at what was going on before 1798, and at the kind of poetry that was being written, read and admired. The real importance of Wordsworth's achievement can only be seen by looking at it from this point of view; what matters most in an appreciation of the *Ballads* is not what followed, but what went before.

THE AUGUSTAN AGE

The eighteenth century was the age of Newton, Swift, Pope, Dr. Johnson. It was a civilized, elegant, scientific age, an age that prized order and solved problems. After the violence and emotions of the Civil War, the nation did its best to avoid the irrational and the extravagant. The mood of the time was urbane and urban; it was during this century that Doctor Johnson, the critic and poet, announced that a man who is tired of London is tired of life, and most well-bred, well-educated people would have agreed with him. The whole culture of the time was centred upon London, and upon the highly civilized life of court. As ever, civilization bred satire, and the greatest writers of the time were also the greatest satirists. As well as the great satirists like Swift and Pope, there were however a whole horde of lesser authors, who seemed to spend their time writing scurrilous attacks upon each other, being witty at each other's expense, and forming themselves into innumerable petty little factions and coteries. As in our modern satirical boom, personalities were all-important; the world was small, inbred, social and malicious. Everybody knew everybody; half the fun of reading poetry lay in trying to guess who was being mocked, and those who were out of touch with the central life of London could hardly be expected to get much pleasure from poems like *The Dunciad* (1728), which is Pope's savage onslaught on the petty journalists and scribblers of the day. Pope was unquestionably the finest poet of the century, and his talent managed to transform even abuse into poetry but, in the hands of lesser authors, abuse remained abuse; the underside of wit is malice, and even a man of Pope's quality could not avoid getting himself involved in the most appallingly vicious and bitter personal squabbles. In this age of polite elegance, a titled poetess, and a woman of great education and intelligence, did not find it beneath her dignity to write about Pope in terms like these, not even sparing the fact that he had a crooked back:

> But, as thou hatest, be hated by mankind,
> And with the emblem of thy crooked mind
> Marked on thy back, like Cain, by God's own hand,
> Wander, like him, accursed through the land.
>> VERSES ADDRESSED TO THE IMITATOR OF THE FIRST
>> SATIRE OF THE SECOND BOOK OF HORACE, Lord Hervey
>> and Lady Mary Wortley Montague

The elegance and the back-biting malice go together; they are the two sides of the same coin.

Not all the poetry of the age, however, was on this dismal and libellous level. At its best it was something very different, and it

22

is only fair to look at the best as well as at the worst. Perhaps the easiest way of showing the qualities of this Augustan poetry, which was so unlike Wordsworth in almost every way, would be to look at a typical piece of Pope, and to see exactly what it is made of, and what it is trying to do. Here is an extract from one of Pope's Epistles, Epistle No. 3, which was written in 1737. It is entitled *The Use of Riches*, and this particular episode tells the story of the miserable death of a famous misuser of riches, George Villiers, the second Duke of Buckingham, who died in a remote inn in Yorkshire at the end of the seventeenth century, having managed to get through a fortune of £50,000 a year.

(Cliveden was one of his stately homes; the Countess of Shrewsbury, whose husband he killed in a duel, was his mistress.)

> Behold what blessings wealth to life can lend!
> And see what comfort it affords our end.
> In the worst inn's worst room, with mat half-hung,
> The floors of plaster, and the walls of dung,
> On once a flock-bed, but repaired with straw,
> With tape-tied curtains never meant to draw,
> The George and Garter dangling from that bed
> Where tawdry yellow strove with dirty red,
> Great Villiers lies—alas! how changed from him,
> That life of pleasure and that soul of whim!
> Gallant and gay, in Cliveden's proud alcove,
> The bower of wanton Shrewsbury and love;
> Or just as gay, at council, in a ring
> Of mimicked statesmen and their merry King.
> No wit to flatter left of all his store!
> No fool to laugh at, which he valued more.
> There, victor of his health, of fortune, friends,
> And fame, this lord of useless thousands, ends.

296-314

This passage illustrates most of Pope's remarkable virtues. It is highly intelligent and serious, yet at the same time cool and witty; it is beautifully balanced, detailed and developed. It is written in the most fashionable verse form of the day, the heroic couplet: that is, in pairs of rhymed lines, each line consisting of five regular iambic feet. Nearly all of Pope is written in this verse form, and it remained by far the most popular form until well on in Wordsworth's lifetime. The passage also contains most of the text-book figures of speech, such as assonance, alliteration, antithesis, bathos and so on, which are associated with this kind of poetry; but it must be noted that, although they are there, they do not stick out uncomfortably; they are part of the poem and its meaning, not just added for decoration. The words themselves are plain and colourful, not vague or artificial; they are all words that might well be used in ordinary conversation. It is quite obvious that the whole passage was written with great care, rather than in a great flow of unchecked inspiration.

It is, in fact, a highly polished piece of work. Its subject is aristocratic—that is, it is about a Duke, not about a shop-keeper or a ploughboy—and its tone is accordingly civilized and worldly, the tone of a gentleman speaking to gentlemen. And yet Pope leaves the reader in no possible doubt about his attitude to the dead Duke of Buckingham. The poet does not approve of the Duke. This is so obvious that we have to look with care to see exactly how we get this impression, for Pope certainly does not descend to vulgar abuse in this particular passage. He starts off, in fact, in what seems to be an approving way:

> Behold what blessings wealth to life can lend!
> And see what comfort it affords our end.

He *seems* here to be saying that wealth *is* a blessing and a comfort, in death as in life, which is indeed what everybody always assumes. But then he goes on, without any comment, to draw his illustration, and the illustration itself opens with the heavy, even beat of a dirge or a dead march:

> In the worst inn's worst room, with mat half hung . . .

Each word, consisting of one heavy single beat, takes us further away from the idea of wealth, blessing and comfort; and the next few lines march inexorably on, filling in all the squalid details, not shying away from words like 'plaster', 'dung', 'flock-bed', and 'straw', until, in the midst of this pitiful, squalid little scene, we suddenly come across the dirty, disgraced red and yellow of the George and Garter, the last thing we might expect to find in such a dumtp, and then, finally, 'Great Villiers himself. Note how the rhyhm builds up to this line; there is' hardly a pause until we get to the words 'Great Villiers lies—', and then there is a complete break, although in the middle of the line. The verse mounts to this point, with a steady beat, and then starts to fall away from it: the passage is neatly separated into two parts—Villiers in the inn, and Villiers as he was once, gallant and gay, surrounded by friends, flatterers and lovers. Note, too, the wonderful irony of the word 'great'; for Villiers is no longer great. He is both poor and dead.

The key to Pope's method is in fact the use of irony. He does not state the obvious; he paints a picture of it, and lets it speak for itself. While seeming to praise, he lets the facts speak; he shows us the tawdry yellow and the dirty red, and sums the whole situation up in one neat final phrase—'this lord of useless thousands'. He does not give a lecture on extravagance; he does everything by implication. His technique is superb and, although he uses every trick, the effect is nevertheless easy and natural. Heroic couplets are one of the most constricting of verse forms, requiring great invention, precision and control, as you will find out if you try to write a few, but Pope manages to give an impression of effortless variety. One of the misfortunes of eighteenth-century poetry was in fact Pope's immense skill and superiority; he brought the heroic couplet to perfection, and he made life very difficult indeed for those who came after him. Various great poets have had an unfortunate effect on their followers and would-be imitators—Milton and Shakespeare, for example, both so outstanding in their own fields, had some disastrous imitators—and Pope was so finished and accomplished a writer that his example tended to deaden rather than encourage others. His rivals and followers could not hope to outdo him; the best they could hope for was to do nearly as well.

Despite his technical brilliance and the highly-polished surface of his poetry, however, Pope was not merely a poet of the surface. His work is far more than a mere string of figures of speech. The romantics in the following century were to accuse him of writing with his head and not with his heart, and certainly he was not given to vague emotional outpourings, but for all that his poetry is neither unemotional nor impersonal. It is cool, but not cold; intelligent, but not dry or mechanical. He cared about what he wrote about; his subject, when all is said, is human nature, human society, and human behaviour. He is deeply concerned about the right way to live, and one of the great strengths of his poetry lies in its closeness to the facts of real life; as he himself said, 'The proper study of mankind is man', and he studied man in all his weaknesses and oddities. Pope is not cut off from, but closely involved in, the life of his times; his poetry shows a very delicate and rare balance of heart and head. However, although he is in many ways typical of the best of eighteenth-century literature, he belongs very much to the first half of the century; he died in 1744, thirty years before Wordsworth's birth, and what happened between Pope and Wordsworth was quite another matter.

END OF THE AUGUSTAN AGE

In the second half of the eighteenth century, something went very wrong with the course of English poetry. We have seen what the ideal qualities of the age were, and some of their dangers: wit that was dangerously near malice, a close connection with daily life that often degenerated into mere scandal and gossip, elegance that sometimes (though never in Pope) became mere outward neatness and artificiality. Towards the end of the century, however, all the virtues of this style were lost, and only its vices were left. The poet gradually backed out of the mainstream of English life, finding it impossible to survive in the atmosphere of literary London, and shut himself up in country churchyards, writing misty, vague, unimportant verse full of words like 'pensive', 'votary', 'mystic' and 'mute'. The typical poet of this period is the English country gentleman or clergyman, gently lamenting the decay of country virtue. In some ways this poet is far more like Wordsworth than Pope was, in subject matter at least, for Wordsworth too was to write about country virtue, though neither gently nor pensively. The heroic couplet of Pope was still widely used, but it had lost almost all its edge and bite. There were of course poets who could still write with keen satirical indignation, like the little-read Crabbe (now perhaps better known because of *Peter Grimes*, Britten's opera), who directed the acid criticism of Pope at country, not city, life; but far more typical of the period are Gray and Goldsmith.

Gray and Goldsmith are not bad poets, but they are what are known as minor poets. Even their best poems show a lack of energy, a softness, a lack of original and powerful feeling. Their writing has a tired note; it feels like the end of something, and not like a new beginning, although it is so different from the sophisticated work of Pope. Gray's *Elegy in a Country Churchyard*, finished in 1750, and Goldsmith's *Deserted Village*, published in 1770, are fascinating examples of what was happening before the *Lyrical Ballads* burst upon the world—fascinating both in their differences and in their similarities. For Wordsworth was to use the same subject matter, almost at times the same attitudes; he too was to write of country churchyards and deserted villages, but the gulf between his achievement and theirs is immense. He is immeasurably superior; in contrast with Gray and Goldsmith, he is immediately recognizable as a major poet.

Both of these earlier poems are in the pastoral tradition: that is, they deal with country life, with shepherds and ploughboys and not with dukes and politicians. They both contain descriptions of nature, of lowing herds winding over the lea, of nodding beeches and smiling plains and mouldering walls. (Mouldering is, typically, another favourite word of the period.) Both poems also contain a good deal of moralizing about the hard lot of the innocent countryman, and praise the simple rural life at the expense of the wicked ways of the city. They are poems of retreat and withdrawal; they reject the sophisticated literary malicious world of Pope, with all its vices and virtues. And yet the kind of country life that they paint is somehow not very real or convincing; it is too poetic, too beautiful, too perfect. The poet's attitude to the 'rustic folk' he writes about is patronizing, and he writes as though he does not really know them; the figures in the poems are not real people, but quaint pretty figures in an artificial landscape. In Wordsworth's pastoral poems, we are in a word of real people, living and suffering, building real sheepfolds and guarding real sheep and burying real corpses in real churchyards. For Gray, however, the churchyard is not so much a real place as an excuse for a few well-chosen and well-expressed platitudes. In the following couple of stanzas, Gray expresses a thought which is in itself commonplace enough, though his words have become famous as a quotation. He is speaking of the unknown people who lie in the graves he is gazing at, and he says:

> Full many a gem of purest ray serene,
> The dark unfathomed caves of ocean bear:
> Full many a flower is born to blush unseen,
> And waste its sweetness on the desert air.

> Some village-Hampden, that with dauntless breast
> The little Tyrant of his fields withstood,
> Some mute inglorious Milton here may rest,
> Some Cromwell guiltless of his country's blood.

ELEGY IN A COUNTRY CHURCHYARD 53-60

The first of these stanzas makes the general moral observation, and its meaning is clear enough, and perfectly acceptable and tastefully expressed. Men, like flowers, sometimes live and die with their virtues unnoticed and unappreciated, the poet says. This is probably true, and certainly not an idea that anyone would quarrel with. But in the second stanza, when he goes on to give particular examples of these hidden 'flowers', his

28

language is not quite so unobjectionable: for some reason he seems to be being patronizing and condescending. If we look closely at what he actually says, we can see that it is words like 'little' and 'dauntless' that do the damage. Why 'little'? The tyrant mentioned was probably not a 'little' tyrant at all, to the man who suffered from his tyranny. The poet calls him little only because he does not take him seriously; he is detached and amused, he is watching the courage of the village labourer not with real attention and interest, but with the detached, kindly amusement of a grown-up watching children at play. He is not really thinking of a man of Milton's power and intellect when he writes of 'some mute inglorious Milton'; he does not really think that the man in the grave before him could have written like Milton if he had been given a chance. His reflections have not got anything to do with the situation or difficulties of those he is talking about; they are the products of fancy, not of hard thought, deep feeling, and true human insight.

When Wordsworth writes about country people, he writes in quite a different manner. He too held that uneducated people, like shepherds, can look at the world with 'a poet's eye', but when he says this he is not indulging in the fancy that they might all be mute inglorious Miltons who have just not had a chance to produce *Paradise Lost*. He does not imagine that the Lake District is peopled with thwarted poets. What he does say is something more serious, and far more probable; he says that even the humblest and least sophisticated of men can have a true sense of the depth and meaning of life, and that the feelings of the humble are as important as those of the most famous and fortunate. The shepherd may be inarticulate, he does not write or read poetry, he may not even know what the word 'poetry' means, but he can still know the sources of poetic feeling in his own heart, even though they are quite different from the poetic feelings of literary people. His knowledge is different from the knowledge of a professional poet like Gray or Goldsmith or Wordsworth, but because it is different it is not necessarily less valuable, and Wordsworth writes of this knowledge not with

29

amused patronage, not as a superior being, but with respect. Of the old shepherd Michael, a man quite insignificant in the eyes of the world, he has this to say:

> No doubt if you in terms direct had asked
> Whether he loved the mountains, true it is
> That with blunt repetition of your words
> He might have stared at you, and said that they
> Were frightful to behold, but had you then
> Discoursed with him in some particular sort
> Of his own business, and the goings on
> Of earth and sky, then truly had you seen
> That in his heart there were obscurities,
> Wonders and admiration, things that wrought
> Not less than a religion in his heart. . . .

From a cancelled draft of MICHAEL

These are the words of someone who really knows country people, and the depths of which they are capable. Wordsworth does not expect these people to be able to talk well, or to understand what a stranger means when he asks them a seemingly useless, meaningless question like 'Do you love the mountains?' You do not find out about these people, Wordsworth says, by asking them literary questions, nor by sitting idly in a graveyard and looking at their tombstones, but by getting to know them, and by knowing about lambing and sheep-dips and snowdrifts and other such ungentlemanlike, unpoetic subjects. It is only by understanding the practical difficulties of a man's way of life that we can understand the man himself, and Gray looks at his humble villagers and rustic ploughboys from a very safe distance.

Goldsmith's attitude to country life, and his use of pastoral poetry are very similar to Gray's, though as a poet he has more genuine warmth. In his poem *The Deserted Village* he laments, as Wordsworth was often to lament, the harsh social changes that were driving the happy villagers from their peaceful homes to seek work in the towns. What he was deploring, though of course he could not see it at the time, was the beginning of the Industrial Revolution itself. He laments with sympathy the misery and poverty that have overtaken the villagers, and paints a glowing, tender and idealized picture of how wonderful life was before. This feeling that the golden age is only just over, that everything was wonderful just a few years ago, is entirely typical of the usual kind of pastoral poetry; Wordsworth is one of the few writers to point out that country life, particularly a shepherd's life, is hard and dangerous, and always has been, and that it is led not necessarily in 'level pastures', but more often amongst 'snows and streams ungovernable', and dismally howling winds. (See *The Prelude, 8,* 353-60.)

Goldsmith's descriptions of his village are more real and detailed than Gray's, but nevertheless one cannot help noticing how much his attitude, too, is that of a superior townsman. One of the main reasons why he regrets that poverty has overtaken and ruined his favourite village is that he had hoped to go and retire there, much as a tired business-man would retire to the country today. He writes of laying himself down 'amid the humble bowers' and showing his book-learning to the swains. Some at least of his feeling about the deserted village are selfish; he writes not as a man who has just lost his job, his land and his money, as the villagers had, but as a rich visitor who finds his favourite view has been spoiled by a quarry or a gas works.

In the poem, Goldsmith draws the characters of various inhabitants of the old, happy, golden-age village; he describes the schoolmaster, the inn keeper, the vicar. His attitude is kindly, without being condescending as Gray is condescending; the characters are types, not individuals, and they are seen through something of a rosy glow of nostalgia, but they are based on some real knowledge and observation. Here is part of Goldsmith's description of the country preacher; it is a good example of a pastoral portrait, and it makes a revealing comparison with Wordsworth's character sketches:

> His house was known to all the vagrant train,
> He chid their wanderings, but relieved their pain;
> The long remembered beggar was his guest,
> Whose beard descending swept his aged breast;

The ruined spendthrift, now no longer proud,
Claimed kindred there, and had his claims allowed;
The broken soldier, kindly bade to stay,
Sate by his fire and talked the night away,
Wept o'er his wounds, or talked of sorrows done,
Shouldered his crutch, and showed how fields were won.
Pleased with his guests, the good man learned to glow,
And quite forgot their vices in their woe;
Careless their merits or their faults to scan,
His pity gave ere charity began.

THE DESERTED VILLAGE, 149-62

This passage, like the one quoted from Pope, is in heroic couplets, but there is little other resemblance. There is none of the careful, mounting excitement of Pope's lines; the rhythm is placid, even and slow. The description has no startling detail, no colour, none of the shocking vividness of the tawdry yellow and the dirty red; the words themselves are vague rather than precise and everyday. At no point does it surprise. It is not compact; the couplet about the ruined spendthrift, for example, could be cut out and never missed, whereas a line out of Pope would unbalance the whole argument. There are no physical details, apart from the vaguest and most general mentions of beards sweeping aged breasts, and the poet tends to use poetic phrases like 'vagrant train', when what he really means is beggars. 'Vagrant train' is not a phrase that anyone would think of using in speech. The characters mentioned are not distinct; the beggar, the spendthrift and the soldier are not individuals; they stand for any beggar, any spendthrift, any soldier. Wordsworth too wrote about almost exactly the same kind of characters; he too wrote about beggars and soldiers, but when we look at his descriptions, we find ourselves in a different world.

WORDSWORTH'S NEW VIEW

In a passage in *The Prelude*, Wordsworth gives his version of the broken soldier. This character was a common enough figure of the times; disbanded soldiers, returned from service abroad, could be seen wandering all the roads of England in search of charity or employment, or on their way back to their homes and native villages. Many of them were wounded and ill; most of them had only joined the army because they could not find work at home, and on their return they found themselves worse off than ever. Wordsworth, who also spent much of his time trudging the highways of England, though for different reasons, must have seen and met many such people, and they figure in various of his poems, such as *The Female Vagrant* and *The Excursion*. In this particular passage of *The Prelude*, he writes of how he saw one of these soldiers while he was taking a walk at night near his home in the Lake District; he was a very young man at the time, not yet twenty, and when he suddenly came upon the soldier in the moonlight he was surprised and alarmed, not having expected to meet anyone at that late hour. He stopped and watched him for some time, himself unseen, before he dared to approach any nearer. Here is his description of the soldier:

> He was of stature tall,
> A foot above man's common measure tall,
> Stiff in his form, and upright, lank and lean;
> A man more meagre, as it seemed to me,
> Was never seen abroad by night or day.
> His arms were long, and bare his hands; his mouth
> Shew'd ghastly in the moonlight: from behind
> A milestone propp'd him, and his figure seem'd
> Half-sitting, and half-standing. I could mark
> That he was clad in military garb,
> Though faded, yet entire. He was alone,
> Had no attendant, neither Dog, nor Staff,
> Nor knapsack; in his very dress appear'd
> A desolation, a simplicity
> That seem'd akin to solitude . . .

THE PRELUDE, *4*, 405–19

Wordsworth watches this strange, awe-inspiring figure in mingled 'fear and sorrow', and listens to him murmuring and groaning quietly to himself. In the end his curiosity and pity overcome his fear, and he plucks up courage to speak to him. The soldier responds to his greeting in this way:

> Slowly from his resting-place
> He rose, and with a lean and wasted arm
> In measur'd gesture lifted to his head,
> Return'd my salutation.

THE PRELUDE, 4, 436–9

The boy asks him his story, and he tells his tale in a 'quiet uncomplaining voice' and with 'a stately air of mild indifference'. He says that he had served in the army in the tropics, and is now on his way home. Wordsworth in the end persuades him to take shelter for the night, instead of staying out in the open, and directs him to a friendly neighbour's cottage.

It is obvious at once that this piece of poetry is very different from the fatherly poetry of Goldsmith. For one thing, this piece tells the tale of one real soldier, whom a real boy really met one night on the road; it is not just the general representative tale of any old 'broken soldier'. For another thing, the soldier is frightening and alarming, not a harmless, pitiable object. The observer, not the soldier, is the one who is ignorant, afraid and inexperienced. The soldier has been through such hardships and seen such sights that he bears the print of them in his whole appearance, and when questioned about his adventures he does not reply with wild romances, nor boast and complain about what has happened to him, as Goldsmith's soldier does. He does not weep and display his crutches and scars; he replies with dignity, without exaggeration or complaint, telling 'in simple words a Soldier's tale'. The whole encounter is impressive and moving, and clearly made a mark on Wordsworth. One can tell at every word that it truly happened, and that he did not just 'make it up'. The episode has the detailed, inconsequential clarity of real life, and is firmly rooted, as are all Wordsworth's best descriptions, in time and place: the still, empty road, the moonlight, the milestone, the grotesque figure of the soldier in his faded uniform—all these things are important parts of the experience. Most important of all, though, is the relationship of soldier and boy; it is not a relationship of mere charity, like that of Goldsmith's preacher and soldier. The boy is in a position to offer help and a night's lodging, but he does not do it in a spirit of condescension or superiority, but timidly and with respect. He is aware, as he makes his offer, of things that had not even crossed Goldsmith's mind; to him the soldier is not an object but a person.

The soldier in *The Prelude* is by no means Wordsworth's only illustration from the band of characters that Goldsmith calls 'the vagrant train'. There are plenty of others which would make interesting comparisons: compare, for instance, Goldsmith's beggar with Wordsworth's poem *The Old Cumberland Beggar*, or with the old man in *Old Man Travelling; Animal Tranquillity and Decay*, both of which poems were to appear in the *Lyrical Ballads*. They are full of a deep feeling for the helplessness and dignity of age, and yet quite without sentimentality. The picture of the old beggar, sitting and eating his scraps, with his hands trembling so much that he cannot help but drop crumbs for the birds, is beautifully observed, with great attention to detail, yet it is a sight that can still be seen on many a park bench today. Much of Wordsworth's originality lies in the fact that he was one of the first writers to pay serious attention to such things, and one of the very few able to turn them into poetry.

WORDSWORTH'S EARLY POEMS

So far we have taken a very quick look at the poetry of the eighteenth century, and now we come to the position in which Wordsworth found himself, as a would-be poet at the end of the century. Pope, the much-admired master of the age, had been dead for years, and none of his imitators in the satirical, elegant tradition of wit were worth very much. The other, pastoral tradition, of which *Elegy in a Country Churchyard* and *The Deserted Village* are the best examples, was nearer to Wordsworth's own interests, and it was in this style that he started to write. But it was not a happy or a stimulating time for poets: most of the verse that was being turned out was far worse than Gray's or Goldsmith's, far more removed from real life, and full of false and emptily poetic phrases. It was almost impossible to write good, serious poetry about anything important; with a few notable eccentric exceptions, like Burns and Blake, the very best that was being written at this time was a kind of minor landscape nature poetry. A young poet in those days had very little to inspire him; the subject matter—dewy evenings, grave-yards, and so on—was extremely limited; the worn-out heroic couplet was still the most usual metre and verse form, though it was being used for all kinds of unsuitable subjects; and the language of poetry was in a shocking state. Poetry, in fact, was in urgent need of a total revolution. Before looking at this revolution, however, perhaps it might be as well to look at the problem of language. One of Wordsworth's strongest objec-tions to eighteenth-century poetry was to its language: to what he called its 'poetic diction'. We must look at what this poetic diction was, before we can see how Wordsworth changed it, and why he felt he had to change it.

There is a sonnet, alleged to be by Wordsworth, which could hardly be more typical of the false poetic diction and the literary vices of the age: it makes a beautiful illustration of how not to write. As a matter of fact the evidence that it really is by Words-worth is very slight indeed, and to me quite unconvincing, though it has been generally accepted as his, and could have been written by him as a very young man; the earliest poems of most writers are usually full of things that would make their older selves blush with shame. This sonnet is called *Sonnet on Seeing Miss Helen Maria Williams Weep at a Tale of Distress* and it was published under a pseudonym in a magazine in 1787 when Wordsworth was seventeen. The subject of the poem is the writer's mighty emotion at the sight of Miss Williams in tears; Miss Williams was a literary lady whom Wordsworth did not in fact meet till many years after the sonnet was written.

Even if the poem is his, this fact can hardly make it more trivial and artificial than it is already.

> She wept. Life's purple tide began to flow
> In languid streams through every thrilling vein;
> Dim were my swimming eyes—my pulse beat slow,
> And my full heart was swelled to dear delicious pain.
> Life left my loaded heart, and closing eye;
> A sigh recalled the wanderer to my breast;
> Dear was the pause of life, and dear the sigh
> That called the wanderer home, and home to rest.
> That tear proclaims—in thee each virtue dwells,
> And bright will shine in misery's midnight hour;
> As the soft star of dewy evening tells
> What radiant fires were drowned by day's malignant power,
> That only wait the darkness of the night
> To cheer the wandering wretch with hospitable light.
>
> AXIOLOGUS

By any standards, this is a very feeble poem. It is hard to follow, and not worth following when one makes the effort. It is highly sentimental; the writer's aim in writing it was probably a desire to flatter Miss Williams, a lady of some influence in literary circles, but unlike the flattery of the early eighteenth century it is quite empty of wit. It is the language, though, that really gives it away. It is full of padding and clichés—phrases like 'life's purple tide' and 'misery's midnight hour' are hardly very original. Evening is 'dewy'; stars are 'radiant'. It is all very poetic and overblown and meaningless; the words are very big, but they do not add up to anything. One would think, from the words alone, that the poem was about something very lofty and important, not about somebody watching somebody else have a little cry. And without the helpful title and the helpful common sense of the first two words, one really would not know what it was about at all. The emotion is as sloppy and vague as the language; the poem is a good illustration of the fact that the more you go on about something, the less likely you are to be believed.

This, then, is one extreme of bad poetic diction; this is the kind of stuff that was being churned out when Wordsworth was a young man. Not all poetry, even in this style, was as bad as this, of course; there were some writers who managed to produce some good and lasting work, even within these conventions and limitations. Wordsworth himself, before he gained the maturity and confidence to defy convention, produced some good examples of conventional verse, as well as this one hypothetical bad example. Even if he had never gone on to write anything else, he would still have a place as the writer of *An Evening Walk* and *Descriptive Sketches*, his earliest published poems, which came out in 1793, five years before the *Lyrical Ballads*. These poems, although there is nothing original or revolutionary about them, are very good of their kind. Here is a passage from *An Evening Walk*, describing a farmyard cock:

> Sweetly ferocious round his native walks,
> Gaz'd by his sister-wives, the monarch stalks;
> Spur-clad his nervous feet, and firm his tread,
> A crest of purple tops his warrior head.
> Bright sparks his black and haggard eye-ball hurls
> Afar, his tail he closes and unfurls;
> Whose state, like pine-trees, waving to and fro,
> Droops and o'er canopies his regal brow,
> On tiptoe rear'd he blows his clarion throat,
> Threat'ned by faintly answering farms remote.

129–38

This is very much better than the sonnet; so much is clear at a glance. The description of the cock is carefully drawn, and it is drawn from life; the phrase 'sister-wives' comes from somebody who knows the sexual habits of poultry, and the last line, about the 'faintly answering farms remote', could never have been made up in the study by a poet who had never been for a country walk and heard the noises of the countryside. There is a nice blend of colour and sound, and phrases like 'sweetly ferocious' and 'nervous feet' show real imagination; they are not just mechanical clichés like 'dear delicious pain' and 'purple thrilling tide'. And yet at the same time nobody would claim that this was a great or important piece of poetry; if Wordsworth had gone on writing like this, he would be no more famous or interesting nowadays than other nature poets—like Dyer, Thompson, Akenside and Cowper. These nature poets are good enough in their way, all of them, but it is no use pretending that they are of much interest today except to students or ardent nature-lovers; they have little appeal to the general reader. And even in this short passage, good though it is, we can see some of the weaknesses of this kind of poetry: the language is slightly artificial, the cock is not spoken of as a cock, but as a 'monarch' with a 'regal brow'. There is a slight touch of mockery, of the mock-heroic which Pope used so wittily. The passage is in heroic couplets, like Pope, but without any real reason; the break between the fifth and sixth lines, for instance, with the word 'afar' dragging over from one line to the next, is not very elegant. Even here, we see the determination not to call a spade a spade, but to call it or to compare it to something else: Cowper, another nature poet of the same kind, calls hens 'the feathered tribe domestic', which is a very roundabout way of saying something very simple. Elsewhere in the *Evening Walk*, which is supposed to be a description of a real evening walk, Wordsworth mentions druids and curfews and hermits, which certainly he could never have seen or heard; it is as though a poet today were to pretend that every English village still has a Maypole and a May Queen, when everyone knows that in most places they haven't been seen for centuries.

This, then, is the situation in which Wordsworth, as a young, original and energetic poet, first started to write. The language of poetry was artificial, and its subjects for the most part trivial. The best that was being produced was landscape and nature poetry; the worst was feeble, sentimental verses about love. The proper study of mankind, which, as Pope said, is Man, was hardly getting any attention at all. Intelligence and humanity had got pushed out of poetry since Pope's day, and an intelligent man who wanted to write about subjects more interesting than poultry, sunsets and gravestones would have to make a whole fresh start. And this is exactly what Wordsworth found himself obliged to do. He did not want to go on writing the kind of thing he was expected to write, so he had to chose the unexpected.

3

The *Lyrical Ballads*

1

We come, at last, to the *Lyrica Ballads* themselves. And we come back to the original questions: What was it about them that was so new? In what ways were they so different from what had gone before? We have seen some of the things they were not; now we must look at what they were.

The *Lyrical Ballads* are different from the kind of poetry we have been examining in almost every way, and certain points are noticeable at the quickest of glances. The briefest of looks through the two editions of 1798 and 1800 will show the most striking new departures.

1. *Metre:* The heroic couplet has gone. Some of the poems are in blank verse, but most of them are in very simple ballad stanzas, with short lines and simple rhymes. This is the kind of verse:

> We walked along, while bright and red
> Uprose the morning sun;
> And Matthew stopped, he looked, and said
> 'The will of God be done!'
>
> THE TWO APRIL MORNINGS, 1–4

2. *Language:* The language too is simple, not poetic, artificial or grandiose. There are no purple, thrilling tides; when Wordsworth means blood, he says blood. Most of the words are in everyday use even today, and many of the poems, like traditional ballads, are made or partly made of conversation. Most of the objects mentioned are homely, and they are called by their

ordinary homely names. In the following few lines, typical of this new language, there is not one word that is hard to understand, and the only figure of speech is a simile comparing one ordinary object to another:

> There is a Thorn—it looks so old,
> In truth, you'd find it hard to say
> How it could ever have been young,
> It looks so old and grey.
> Not higher than a two years' child
> It stands erect, this agèd Thorn . . .

THE THORN, I–6

3. *Subject Matter:* These poems are not nature poetry or landscape poetry. Most of them are about people, but they are not about aristocrats, like the dead Duke of Buckingham, nor about literary ladies like Miss Helen Maria Williams. They are about ordinary people and poor people and country people, with names like Michael and Susan and Simon Lee. Where there are slight resemblances in setting or subject matter, the resemblance is wholly superficial; we have already seen how different a poem like *The Old Cumberland Beggar* is from Goldsmith's *Deserted Village*, although that has beggars in it too. Another of the ballads, *We are Seven*, is set in or near a country churchyard, but it has no other possible connection with any other poem by Gray. This difference of subject matter is clearly at the root of the whole matter; simple things must be written about in simple verse.

We now come back to the next of our original questions. Granted that the *Lyrical Ballads* are new in both style and subject, is this difference deliberate and intentional, or is it accidental? And if it is intentional, what are the intentions behind it?

The difference is, of course, intentional in every way. This highly revolutionary volume of poetry is not the product of an inspired innocent, of some uneducated primitive genius of the backwoods, nor of a man so ignorant that he just did not know how most poets wrote poetry. It is the product of two highly intelligent, conscious, deliberate artists, who knew exactly what they wanted to do, and who knew exactly how shocking and unconventional their aims were. Both ordinary readers and professional critics were taken aback when confronted with this small anonymous collection of verse, in 1798, and hardly knew what to make of it, but this was exactly what Wordsworth and Coleridge intended. They published anonymously partly because they wished to surprise; they did not want anyone to compare this new volume with their own earlier, more traditional poetry. They were, in their own words, making an experiment; they knew quite well that they were ahead of—or at least out of line with—public taste, and they wanted to see what would happen, and how many people would take them seriously.

The gesture which they made could be compared, in our own century, to the gesture against orthodox taste which T. S. Eliot made, when he published his first volume of poetry in 1917; in many ways the situation of Wordsworth and Coleridge was similar to Eliot's at the beginning of this century. He, like them, was brought up in a period of very bad, stagnant, uninteresting poetry, and his age, like theirs, had been violently upset by a great outside force—in their case the French Revolution, in his the First World War. Eliot was the poet of the postwar world; he created a new style, a whole new way of writing, which brought poetry back into touch with real life, and which set free whole generations of writers after him. When he wrote, in a serious poem, a line like:

I shall wear the bottoms of my trousers rolled

or used a simile like:

The evening is spread out against the sky
Like a patient etherized upon a table

THE LOVESONG OF J. ALFRED PRUFROCK

he was making a gesture very like Wordsworth's; he was using

43

new words, new images, new subject matter, and one of his reasons for doing so was a desire to shock people out of their boredom with poetry. He knew quite well that the average reader, looking at a pageful of verse about nooks and brooks, fires and desires, was filled with boredom, or at the most with polite, unenthusiastic respect, and he wanted to make his readers wake up and pay attention. Wordsworth's intentions were very similar; he knew that the old way was worn out and out of touch, and he wanted to bring freshness and directness back into poetry, after their long absence.

THE 'PREFACE' OF 1800

We know a good deal about Wordsworth's aims in publishing the *Ballads*, because he tells us about them himself, in a way that leaves no possible doubt about his awareness of what he was doing. The first volume of 1798 was published with a short foreword, in which he states, very briefly, the main points of his argument; the second edition was published in 1800, with many new poems added, and a much longer and more detailed *Preface*. This *Preface* is one of the masterpieces of English criticism; it is intelligent, subtle, yet extremely clear and provocative. Before tackling it, however, it is a good idea for anyone to read the foreword to the first edition; it is only a few hundred words long and can be read in a few minutes, and moreover it is the best possible introduction to the more detailed argument of the longer Preface. It makes, very simply, the following points.

1. The subject matter of poetry is whatever interests the human mind (that is, if a thing is interesting, it does not mean anything at all to say that it is 'undignified' or 'unpoetic').

2. The *Lyrical Ballads* are written as experiments, to try out the use of the language of conversation of real people in poetry.

3. They are new and unusual, and will not 'suit the taste' of most readers.

4. Nevertheless, the reader is asked to try them with an open mind, and not to be put off at first sight without giving them a fair trial.

These same points are the basis of the argument of the longer *Preface*, which, however, is far more fully illustrated, and far more complicated in its ideas. In it, he takes a close look at the 'gaudiness and inane phraseology' of the fashionable poetry of the time, with examples from Gray and Johnson; he says that he has used language and situations from 'low and rustic life' because in low and rustic life man is more simple, more direct, nearer to his own elemental passions, and less affected and artificial in the way he expresses his passions. The language of poetry, he says, should not be different from the language of prose; there is nothing 'special' about poetry, that requires the use of a special language. In the same way, poetry does not require specifically 'poetic' subjects; it does not deal with the grand or the dignified or the sensational, but with the permanent, enduring interests of the human heart—with:

> storm and sunshine, with the revolution of the seasons, with cold and heat, with loss of friends and kindred, with injuries and resentment, gratitude and hope, with fear and sorrow. These, and the like, are the sensations and objects which the Poet describes, as they are the sensations of other men, and the objects which interest them.

In other words, the poet is not a man in an ivory tower, writing about subtle emotions beyond the reach of common people, but a man amongst men, writing about what interests all mankind. Wordsworth writes with evident passion; he feels deeply about his statements, as well as thinking clearly about them.

> Poetry (he says, finely and resonantly) sheds no tears 'such as angels weep', but natural and human tears; she can boast of no celestial ichor that distinguishes her vital juices from those of prose; the same human blood circulates through the veins of both.

The poet, he says, in a phrase that reminds us of Pope's

45

remark that the proper study of mankind is man, is 'a man speaking to men'. Clearly, Wordsworth's feelings about poetry are as much to do with his feelings about humanity and society, as they are to do with a system of aesthetics.

However, he does not leave us with the idea that the poet is merely an ordinary man; he does not believe that anyone can sit down and write great poetry if he happens to feel like it. He says that although the poet feels for man, and about man, and should write in a way that is understandable by most men, he is also possessed of special powers of communication, memory and passion. At several points in the *Preface* he attempts to define what makes a poet write poetry and some of his phrases, such as 'emotion recollected in tranquillity' and 'the spontaneous overflow of powerful feelings' have become deservedly famous; he is one of the first writers to attempt to describe the inner creative process. Perhaps his best and clearest definition of the poet, however, is of the man 'who, being possessed of more than usual organic sensibility, has also thought long and deeply'; a good poet is not first of all a thinker and philosopher, nor is he first of all a sensitive soul pouring forth his own passions. He must unite the two qualities of thought and feeling; the one will not work without the other. He is different from other men not in the *kind* but in the *degree* of his qualities, and it is this extra gift, this extra sensitive intelligence, that makes him able to write about things that other men only dimly feel.

It is quite impossible to try to give an account of all the questions raised by the *Preface*, for in it Wordsworth covers an enormous stretch of ground, throwing out quite effortlessly the most acute observations on the relationship of poetry and science, on the use of metre, on the place of pleasure in art, on Aristotle, on taste and its cultivation, and on the history of poetry. It raises, in fact, almost every knotty aesthetic problem one can think of, and deals with them with an amazing confidence and energy; after reading it, one is quite convinced that Wordsworth at least had thought long and deeply, and that, as he says at the outset, 'indolence' is the last thing he could possibly be accused of. It is a pleasure to read someone who is so sure of his own mind, and who at the same time has nothing dry or opinionated about him; the *Preface* leaves a final impression of a quite extraordinary combination of creative and critical power, of passion and thought. It cannot be read too often; every time it seems to contain something new and unexpected. It marks the beginning of a new age.

SUCCESS OF THE 'LYRICAL BALLADS'

We have seen what Wordsworth's aims were when he wrote the *Lyrical Ballads*. It remains to see how far he succeeded in fulfilling them. Are they too much of an experiment? Did the experimenter get the better of the creative poet, or did the poetry run away with the experiment, or did he achieve the balance that he intended?

Until recently, it has been common to regard Wordsworth's early ballads as examples of well-meaning but ill-guided zeal in the cause of realism. He meant well, critics and readers have agreed, but he went too far. In trying to write poetry about simple things in simple, unaffected language, he exaggerated his intentions so much that he ended up by writing about childish things in childish language. Ever since they were first published, it has been fashionable to laugh at most of the 'simple' poems, like *The Idiot Boy* and *We are Seven*. Certain lines from *The Thorn*:

> I've measured it from side to side
> 'Tis three feet long, and two feet wide

—and from *Simon Lee*:

> For still, the more he works, the more
> His poor old ankles swell

—must be amongst the most ridiculed in the whole of English literature and, in fact, after years of mockery and good advice from friends, Wordsworth actually gave in and altered the first of them to:

> Though but of compass small, and bare
> To thirsty suns and parching air

—which for some reason was thought to be better, as poetry. The usual verdict on poems like these is that Wordsworth only wrote really well when he forgot his own theories about 'poetic diction', and stopped trying to prove the points made in the *Preface*—when, in fact, his heart ran away with his head. This is the usual explanation of what happened in *Tintern Abbey*, which is almost the only poem in the two editions to have a highly elevated, grand poetic style, and which, incidentally, is almost the only poem to show Wordsworth as a 'nature poet'. As proof that Wordsworth is a true traditional poet, capable of finer things than verses on swelling ankles, these lines from *Tintern Abbey* are often quoted:

> And I have felt
> A presence that disturbs me with the joy
> Of elevated thoughts; a sense sublime
> Of something far more deeply interfused,
> Whose dwelling is the light of setting suns,
> And the round ocean and the living air,
> And the blue sky, and in the mind of man:
> A motion and a spirit, that impels
> All thinking things, all objects of all thought,
> And rolls through all things . . .

93–102

Those who ridicule *Simon Lee* and *The Thorn* turn with relief to this kind of passage, and ask triumphantly, is *this* the language of the lower and middle classes? Are these thoughts taken from commonplace country life? Clearly they are not; they are another kind of poetry altogether. But it must be made plain that *Tintern Abbey* is not at all representative of the *Lyrical Ballads* as a whole; it is a freak, and very much in a minority. It is a fine poem, and has always been popular and readily accepted, but this does not mean that all the other poems in the book are bad; if it did, the *Lyrical Ballads* and their *Preface* would not be very important. *Tintern Abbey* may be good, but in many ways it is less entirely successful than the simpler ballads.

Because it is the simplest poems that are most often misunderstood and disliked, and because they show most clearly what Wordsworth was about, it is worth while looking at a few of them.

'WE ARE SEVEN' AND 'ANECDOTE FOR FATHERS'

Both these poems are on the subject of childhood. Wordsworth wrote a good deal about the experiences of childhood; his own was peculiarly important to him, as we know from *The Prelude*. He was also interested in the helpless simplicity of the very young, as he was in the helpless dignity of the very old; childhood, like old age, is one of the experiences that everyone must go through, and it is therefore relevant and interesting to everyone. Some of his critics have seized on these poems about childhood, and used them as evidence that his verse was itself childish, but it does not take much intelligence to see the difference between writing *about* children and writing *childishly*. His poems are not even childlike, as some of Blake's poems, for instance, are; they are always written entirely from the adult's point of view. Although these two poems are simple and straightforward, they are also mature; they are based on an adult's observation, not on the poet's own childhood memories. Some of their admirers have misunderstood them almost as much as their most violent critics, and have overloaded them with all kinds of pretentious hidden meanings that they were never intended to bear. What the poems say is in fact easy enough to follow.

We Are Seven tells of Wordsworth's chance meeting with a little girl, aged about eight. It was a real meeting, as we know from his letters, and he met her while on one of his walking tours in the west of England. She was a real little girl. The poet stops to talk to her, and asks her, idly, as adults always ask children, how many brothers and sisters she has. She replies that she is one of seven, but it emerges, while they chat, that two of these seven are dead. The poet tries, naturally enough, to point out to her that if two are dead, that leaves five, not seven, but the little girl refuses to take his point, and goes on stubbornly insisting that there are seven of them. To most readers, this poem appears to be so much childish nonsense, trivial, repetitive, boring and pointless. The few who have tried to defend it have written either of the little girl's 'natural piety', or of some mystic notion about the child's instinctive knowledge of the immortality of the soul, but this is not what interests Wordsworth at all. What interests him is the child's amazing matter-of-factness, her extraordinary prosaic health. She is just not interested in the idea of death. The first verse states the theme, idly, conversationally, without any hint of pseudo-philosophy:

> A simple child, dear brother Jim,
> That lightly draws its breath,
> And feels its life in every limb,
> What should it know of death?

The child is so alive, she takes living so much for granted, that the idea of death does not disturb her at all. There is nothing virtuous in this, nothing good or Christian or pious on the child's part; it is just a fact. The little girl treats the whole affair with great nonchalance, without fear and without sorrow; this is how she relates the death of the second of the family, one sister being already dead:

> Together round her grave we played,
> My brother John and I.
> And when the ground was white with snow,
> And I could run and slide,
> My brother John was forced to go,
> And he lies by her side.

The death of her brother, fond though she had been of him, clearly did not upset her very much; her mind was at least as much on the memory of playing in the snow as on the memory of his death. The poet, amazed and slightly shocked by her careless attitude, makes a final effort to convince her; we can hear in the tone and rhythm of the verse the adult's slight irritation, his threatening exasperation:

'How many are you, then,' said I,
If they two are in heaven?'
The little maiden did reply,
'O Master! we are seven.'

'But they are dead; those two are dead!
Their spirits are in heaven!'
'Twas throwing words away; for still
The little Maid would have her will,
And said, 'Nay, we are seven!'

Noticeably, it is the poet who uses pious phrases about 'heaven' and 'spirits', not the child. The child is not interested in heaven; the thought of heaven never even crosses her mind. The poet, however, is not trying to say that the child's attitude is *right* and the adult's *wrong*; on the contrary, both poet and reader know that death *is* final, death *is* separation, and it is the child's lack of awareness that makes the poem so touching. When she is older, she will know; she cannot go on with this happy ignorance for ever. Wordsworth does not even claim that all children think this way about death—some children react in a completely different way, with morbid terror and fear—he is telling us about this particular child, and the things that she said to him.

The poem is, I think, a successful poem. It is peculiarly unforgettable; even those who remember it only to ridicule cannot help but remember. Its secret lies not in any deep philosophical statement, but in its accidental, inconsequential note of truth—while reading it, we are convinced that the child did see things that way, that she did say what the poet says she said, and her attitude casts a new and revealing light on our own attitudes to death and the finality of death. Wordsworth had a special talent for catching such accidental moments, such odd quirks of conversation; his poetry is full of chance remarks of total strangers which have happened to impress him. A remark overheard on a train, a comment made by a waiter or a shop-keeper—nothing is too trivial for attention, and truths can be heard in the most unexpected places.

Wordsworth knew quite well that *We Are Seven* was an oddity as a poem, even by his own standards, but as usual at this time in his life, he had a supreme confidence in his own judgment. When a close and well-meaning friend tried to persuade him not to include it in the volume, convinced that it could only harm his reputation and make him 'everlastingly ridiculous', he replied mildly and firmly that it could take its chance. It has taken its chance, and, although it has taken many a beating, it has survived.

Anecdote for Fathers is a similar poem; it too is about the nature of childhood, and about the gap between the adult's view and the child's. In it, as in the other poem, we see the adult Wordsworth earnestly questioning a small child, not this time a stranger, but the little five-year-old boy, Basil Montague, son of a widowed friend of his, whom William and Dorothy helped to bring up. As the boy and the poet take their usual morning walk, the poet idly asks the boy whether he would rather be where he is, at Liswyn farm, or at Kilve by the sea where they had been the spring before. As any parent would have known, this was a silly question, as children invariably say they would rather have what they have not got, and would rather be where they are not; and, sure enough, the boy replies that he would rather be at Kilve. Foolishly, the poet insists: he asks *why* he would rather be at Kilve. The child, of course, has no idea why, and says so. With most unwise persistence the poet goes on repeating his question, until finally the child, in exasperation, makes up an answer, any old answer, just to keep the adult quiet. He'd rather be at Kilve because there's no weather cock there, he says, saying the first thing that comes into his head, as the weather cock catches his eye. The sub-title of the poem is 'Shewing how the art of lying may be taught'; it could equally well be, to use a more modern phrase, 'Showing how a silly question gets a silly answer'. The whole poem is a joke by Wordsworth against Wordsworth; it is slight, non-serious, but entirely accurate and true to human nature, and it catches a kind of domestic, human moment of truth that had never been dealt with in poetry before. The whole relationship of child and adult is there, down to the way the poet 'took him by the arm' . . . 'and held him by the arm' . . . 'while *still* I held him by the arm'—we can almost see the boy struggling to be off. And when Wordsworth says:

Five times did I say to him
'Why, Edward? Tell me why?'

—we know quite well that after those five times the adult deserves what is coming to him, and he gets it in a reply of dazzling inconsequence. The poet ruefully acknowledges his lesson in the last stanza:

Oh dearest, dearest boy! my heart
For better lore would seldom yearn,
Could I but teach the hundredth part
Of what from thee I learn.

What he had learned was of course nothing to do with weather cocks, but that it is dangerous to ask too many questions: one could go on to propound a whole theory about the way that adults corrupt the unthinking simplicity of childhood, but it is hardly necessary. When all is said, it is a slight poem, but it is a good one, unaffected, affectionate and humble. And in it Wordsworth was doing what he set out to do; he was writing in a simple, conversational way of basic, simple things, which is surely much better and more interesting than to write in a grandiose, affected manner about nothing at all. Both these poems on childhood have the ring of first-hand knowledge, and they say things about childhood that, however obvious, had hardly ever been said in verse before. It is also worth noticing that in both poems Wordsworth is not the superior teacher, the moral lawgiver that he is so often thought to be, and which he did later become, but a curious, interested, eager observer, quite ready to learn even from little children, and with far more curiosity than adult dignity.

If *Anecdote for Fathers* and *We Are Seven* are successes on a small and unpretentious scale, *The Idiot Boy* is a triumph by any standards. In it, Wordsworth combined the various aims he set himself with ease and confidence and evident enjoyment; it was always one of his own favourites, and he enjoyed writing it. The older he grew, the more disagreeable the task of writing became to him, and eventually he began to develop all kinds of physical symptoms whenever he got down to work—headaches, pains in the eyes, even pains in the feet. But when he wrote *The Idiot Boy*, he wrote with real pleasure, and his pleasure comes across very strongly. It is not a comic poem or a witty poem—Wordsworth was never very interested in the comic, being the least frivolous of men—but it has a driving force behind it, and a vigorous energy that is very rare in his later work.

It illustrates most of the main points of Wordsworth's poetic manifesto, and some of them are seen in it in an extreme form. It is in a simple, popular ballad metre, like many of the other poems in the volume, and the rhymes are simple and repetitive, sometimes even crude, like those of a street song. The language too is simple and conversational. The second verse shows quite clearly all these points:

> Why bustle thus about your door,
> What means this bustle, Betty Foy?
> Why are you in this mighty fret?
> And why on horseback have you set
> Him whom you love, your Idiot Boy? 7–11

The tone is of a chatty, simple person, asking obvious questions; the rhymes too are obvious, and the rhyme of *Betty Foy* and *Idiot Boy* is one that will be used again and again in the rest of the poem. Even the phrases are colloquial; 'this mighty fret' is a phrase that we would now call slang.

The story, as well as the style, fulfils Wordsworth's aims perfectly. It is a story of 'low and rustic life', but it is exciting and interesting in itself, and shows us the emotions of ordinary people when they are in the grip of strong passion—in this case, when they are threatened by illness and accident. It has suspense, yet it is not artificial. The events, even if not the events of everyday, are perfectly plausible and convincing. It is, however, the subject matter and story of this poem that have made it so notorious, and which have aroused so much angry discussion. It is not the fact that the characters are country people that has been found so objectionable, though this in itself annoys some readers; it is the fact that Wordsworth was able to write, in a perfectly naturalistic manner, about a mentally defective child. In doing this, he really was breaking new ground, and whether he was right or not to go so far has been a matter for discussion ever since he did it. Many people have thought that Wordsworth, in an attempt to avoid the grand, the literary and the aristocratic, had this time really overreached himself, and produced a poem that could only cause disgust. People do not want to read about idiots; they would rather forget their existence. An idiot boy may be the logical opposite of sophisticated decadent dukes and literary ladies, but that does not mean that we want to read about one. Wordsworth's own arguments from the *Preface* have been used against him on this score; in the *Preface*, Wordsworth attacks the use of sensational stories and subjects, saying that the human mind can be moved and interested without the use of 'gross and violent stimulants', and what, say his critics, is the use of an idiot boy but as a gross and violent stimulant? Surely, they say, it is just as disgusting a subject, just as far removed from the sights of daily life, as the murders and headless monks in the Gothic novels which Wordsworth disliked so much. (These Gothic novels, by writers such as Monk Lewis and Mrs. Radcliffe, abound in sensational objects like headless monks, dwarfs and hunchbacks; the word 'Gothic' means medieval or barbarous, and most of these novels are set against macabre medieval backgrounds.) These critics class the use of an idiot boy with the use of Gothic horrors; the subject of the poem is, they say, unnecessarily sensational, like the subjects of horror films today.

The question of sensationalism in art and literature is a tricky one, and one that is always being raised. There are some who think that the use or description of any kind of horror or violence is in bad taste, and has a bad rather than a good effect on the reader. There are others who argue that the use of violence is perfectly permissible as long as it is carefully controlled and directed towards a moral end: for example, to prove that violeuce is a Bad Thing. Clearly there are points on both sides—Shakespeare's *King Lear*, for instance, shows both physical violence (blinding, hanging, poisoning) and idiocy (Lear, the Fool, Edgar) without any indulgence, but, on the other hand, Jacobean drama with its tales of rape, revenge, incest and torture lets these things get quite out of hand. The borderline between the right and wrong use of them will always be disputed; there is no clear dividing line. What is astonishing, however, is that anyone should think that Wordsworth's *Idiot Boy* could fall on the wrong side of any possible line—anyone, that is, who has read it with attention, and not merely glanced at the title.

Wordsworth keeps, as he intended to, as far as can be imagined from sensationalism. It is quite true that certain of his subjects—the Idiot Boy, the Mad Mother, the infanticidal mother of *The Thorn*, the distracted Ruth, the *Female Vagrant*—do have certain similarities with some of the stuff of melodrama, but though the stuff may be the same, the treatment could hardly be more different. It is almost beyond comparison. Wordsworth's aim in writing about these unfortunate outcasts of society is not to shock, not to alarm, not to give us a horrid thrill of supernatural fear and delight, but to show us precisely how normal and unalarming and human these creatures are. He is not saying 'Look at that horrid spectacle', but 'Look how like that creature is to yourself, and do not shrink away'. He writes of the mad mother and the mother by the Thorn with a profound and touching simplicity; they are mad indeed, but no monsters. He shows us not how different they are, but how human they are; even in such a wild-looking, demented sun-tanned being as the mad mother, the instinct of normal motherly love will survive.

He shows us not her madness, but her normality; not her violence, but her tenderness. Yet even his description of her tenderness managed to offend, and the reference to the baby sucking at her breast was considered by some to be most unladylike. Times have changed; it is doubtful whether many people could manage to be shocked by such a reference today. This is a good example of what Wordsworth calls 'false delicacy'; it is not really natural to be shocked by a mention of breasts and babies—it is an affectation.

In the same way, one of the main aims of the *Idiot Boy* is to show us the unreality of our stock reactions to idiots. Wordsworth describes to us the completely natural, affectionate care of Betty Foy for her child; the little country community in which she lived saw nothing shocking or disgusting in him at all. He was completely accepted, and she loved him as she would have loved any other child—more, perhaps, because he was more dependent on her love. To the sophisticated, wealthy city-dweller, the sight of an idiot is perhaps alarming, because rare; most rich people shut their defective relatives up in institutions, to keep them out of the way. Country people cannot on the whole afford to do this, or could not in Wordsworth's day, so defective children were brought up as part of the family, and indeed were often treated with a special care by the whole village—they were a familiar part of the landscape, and the village idiot would belong to the village as did the village postman or the village policeman. Even today, this tradition has not died out; there are still plenty of village idiots left.

It was this natural acceptance of oddity that Wordsworth had in mind when he wrote the poem. From the very first, he makes clear Betty Foy's immense pride and delight in her child; he is her only child, born to her late in life, and she is devoted to him. The story of the poem is very short and uncomplicated; it tells of the night when Betty sends her boy off to town on the pony to fetch the doctor for her sick neighbour, Susan Gale. The boy sets off safely, but does not return, and after a while Betty, who has been sitting up with old Susan, gets into a panic and goes out to look for him. After searching for a long time, she finds him still sitting on the pony, his errand completely forgotten; she brings him home, overcome with relief, and finds that in her absence Susan has recovered, and no longer needs the doctor. The incident is ordinary enough; what distinguishes it is the warmth and insight with which it is narrated. The poet understands the feelings of Betty and of her child; the child is excited by this unexpected adventure, and full of pride at being allowed out at night by himself.

> His heart it was so full of glee
> That, till full fifty yards were gone,
> He quite forgot his holly whip,
> And all his skill in horsemanship;
> Oh! happy, happy, happy John.

82–6

He is delighted to be able to be of use, and he sets off full of a sense of his own importance. Betty, too, has a touching confidence in his reliability; she is at first quite sure he will be able to manage it.

> And Betty's standing at the door,
> And Betty's face with joy o'erflows,
> Proud of herself, and proud of him,
> She sees him in his travelling trim,
> How quietly her Johnny goes.
>
> The silence of her Idiot Boy,
> What hope it sends to Betty's heart . . .

86–92

She watches him till he is out of sight, then goes back to watch and wait for the doctor's arrival with old Susan. The scene between the two neighbours, as they wait, and as it gets later and later, and clearer and clearer that Johnny has got lost, is beautifully written. Betty at first is overflowing with pride; the pony is safe, Johnny is safe, they will be back soon:

　　　　　. . . she,
You plainly in her face may read it,
Could lend out of that moment's store
Five years of happiness or more
To any that might need it . . .

132–5

Then, as time draws on, she starts to listen for his return; she hears all sorts of strange noises, and although at first she will not share her fears with Susan, Susan becomes aware of them. By twelve she 'is not quite at ease', and she starts to relive her anxiety by abusing her boy, labelling him 'a little, idle sauntering thing'. As her anxiety increases, however, she loses all her annoyance, and is overcome by worry, which drives all thought of reproach from her. Both she and Susan recognize that, despite Susan's illness, Betty's first duty is to look for Johnny, and off she goes, leaving Susan to fend for herself. In fact, when she gets to the doctor's and finds Johnny is not there, she is so preoccupied with her own worry that she completely forgets to tell him to go and visit Susan, and on the way there had even got round to abusing Susan for being ill in the first place:

At poor old Susan then she railed,
While to the town she posts away;
'If Susan had not been so ill,
Alas! I should have had him still,
My Johnny, till my dying day.'

232–6

This is not the portrait of a super-virtuous, super self-sacrificing woman, but of a perfectly ordinary, simple, good, well-meaning country woman, who does her best to help her neighbour and her boy, but does not act particularly wisely, however well she means. It is not an idealized portrait; it makes no attempt to portray Betty as a model mother, or a saint of womanhood. Instead it is true to life, and it is convincing. The picture of Susan Gale, though far less detailed, is convincing too, for she, once she is left alone without anyone to complain to,

and at the mercy of her anxieties about Johnny and Betty, starts
to recover:

> As her mind grew worse and worse,
> Her body—it grew better.

415–16

This is no fairy story miracle, but a perfectly plausible and
truthful description of what happens to a person when one
worry displaces another; nobody worries about the toothache
if his house is on fire. The passions of all the characters are
neither exalted nor exaggerated, but true to reality.

Thus the emphasis of the whole poem is on the ordinary and
the natural, not on the weird and the nasty and the supernatural.
It is a tale of ordinary human kindness and silliness. When, in
the descriptions of Johnny's solitary wanderings, the poet has
an opportunity for ghostly Gothic romancing, he deliberately
turns his back on it; he refuses to indulge in the horrid. The
furthest that he goes in this direction is to give a fanciful account
of what *might* have been happening, if the story had been a
supernatural one and not a real one, but the whole of this part of
the poem is done with a kind of mockery:

> Perhaps, and no unlikely thought!
> He with his Pony now doth roam
> The cliffs and peaks so high that are,
> To lay his hands upon a star,
> And bring it in his pocket home . . .
> Perhaps, with head and heels on fire,
> And like the very soul of evil,
> He's galloping away, away . . .

317–21

Of course, we know and the poet knows that nothing of the sort
is happening; we are very soon brought back to earth. Betty,
after long and frantic searches, comes across her boy on the
stolid little pony, not galloping madly across the hilltops, but
standing stockstill by the waterfall. At once we are brought back
to reality; all Betty's terrors vanish, and with them all ghostly

60

possibilities. She sees at once how foolish her panic had been, for 'the pony's worth his weight in gold'; the pony at least is reliable, she should have known that all would be well. Wordsworth makes it quite clear that everything is entirely natural, entirely of this world; he mocks at the tales we read of 'in romances', and says of the idiot boy, 'It is no goblin, 'tis no ghost'—it is only Johnny, sitting here quite unperturbed upon his pony, quite unaware of all the trouble he has caused.

On the way back home, Betty asks her son what he did and saw on his travels. His reply is worth more as poetry than any sensational, frightening descriptions could have been worth; he says, quite simply, thinking of the owls and the moon:

> 'The cocks did crow to-whoo, to-whoo,
> And the sun did shine so cold!'
> Thus answered Johnny in his glory,
> And that was all his travel's story.

> 450–4

These two lines of the idiot boy have the most extraordinary power and magic, not because they are weird and fantastic, but because they are so hard and homely and real and clear; they reveal at one stroke the night-time world, seen in terms of the day, suddenly, shockingly, upside down. It is a perfect example of what Coleridge was to call 'the sense of novelty and freshness with old and familiar objects'; Johnny, we remember, had hardly ever seen the night, had probably never been allowed out after dark alone before, and in these few words of his we have the sudden, piercingly clear vision of the innocent, of a man looking at something for the very first time and telling the truth about what he sees. These lines are the poem's poetic centre; when we come to them, at the end of the low-keyed, homely ballad, we see that they are the spark that kindled the whole imaginative effort. They show an imagination that is in no way ethereal or fantastic; the Wordsworthian imagination, at its most powerful, is peculiarly of this world.

The Idiot Boy, then, is about simplicity and innocence. The subject was one on which Wordsworth had thought, as he says the poet must think, 'both long and deeply'; the poem may appear easy and even crude at times, but its easy flow is the result not of carelessness but of hard work. We have already seen how it fulfils certain of the aims laid down in the *Preface*, in a very clear and decided way; we might end with a look at the way in which it fulfils another aim not yet touched upon. In the *Preface*, Wordsworth says that each of his poems is written with a purpose. However trivial a poem may seem, he says, it has a moral behind it, which can be found if people care to look. The purpose behind this particular poem is partly at least a desire to make people think and feel more humanely about idiot boys, and to show that they have their place in society, and are a cause of as much joy as sorrow; in expressing these notions, Wordsworth was years ahead of his time, and they do show a superior and more kindly morality than that of most people. In a letter to John Wilson, written in 1802, Wordsworth makes a very eloquent and moving defence of the poem, answering many of the usual objections against it; anyone who doubts that Wordsworth did think very seriously and intelligently about his simple tales would do well to read it. After asserting that the disgust caused by the subject of his poem is the result of 'false delicacy' and not of true feeling, he concludes in these stirring words:

> I have, indeed, often looked upon the conduct of fathers and mothers of the lower classes of society towards idiots as the great triumph of the human heart. It is there that we see the strength, disinterestedness and grandeur of love; nor have I ever been able to contemplate an object that calls out so many excellent and virtuous sentiments without finding it hallowed thereby, and having something in me which bears down before it, like a deluge, every feeble sensation of disgust and aversion.

Note that Wordsworth, reasonable and practical as ever, does not deny that digust and aversion are a *possible* reaction; what he does say, quite bluntly and firmly, is that they are wrong. This is a moral attitude; this is the moral of the poem, and it is one which, in this age of mental homes and institutions, where the insane are kept out of sight, is well remembered.

THE LYRICS

The three poems which we have looked at so far (*We Are Seven, Anecdote for Fathers* and *The Idiot Boy*) are all ballads, and all come from the earlier, 1798, edition of the *Lyrical Ballads*. This is no coincidence, as nearly all the most deliberately experimental poems are to be found in the earlier edition: as well as these three there are also *The Thorn, Simon Lee, The Last of the Flock*, and Coleridge's *Ancient Mariner*, all poems which illustrate very clearly the original intentions of the two poets. In contrast, the second edition (1800), which is very much longer, has a much higher lyrical content, and the narrative poems which it does add tend to be less bald and provocative in style: *Michael* and *The Brothers*, for instance, although they too deal with simple, true, country stories, are far less simple and more dignified in expression than *The Idiot Boy*. It is as though Wordsworth, having stated his poetic creed in the 1798 poems, then found himself free to develop and explore its implications; the second edition poems and *Preface* are less dogmatic, more subtle and flexible than the first edition poems and *Foreword*.

In the short space of time between the two editions, Wordsworth was in fact starting to change direction as a poet. He was beginning to move away from simple, objective story-telling towards a more personal kind of poetry, an inner, soul-searching poetry, which was finally to produce that most personal and introspective of all poems, *The Prelude*. He did continue to write ballads, some of which, like *Alice Fell*, appeared as late as 1807, but the later ones lack the direct power and attack of the very early experiments.

It is not of course possible to divide the poems in the *Lyrical Ballads* into two neat groups—ballads and lyrics; the very title of the collection proves this. Basically, a ballad is a simple poem with a story, told in a popular fashion, whereas a lyric is a short poem of personal feeling; part of Wordsworth's and Coleridge's experiment was an attempt to combine the qualities of both forms, by fitting delicate personal emotion to a simple four-line stanza, and by giving emotional attitudes a narrative setting. None of the poems is a mere list of events, and none of them is an outpouring of vague, highly-coloured feeling. However, most of them show some leanings towards one form or the other; in some, like *The Idiot Boy*, the narrative is predominant, whereas in many of the poems which were written after 1798 there is hardly any story at all. It is this second group that we must now consider.

Perhaps the most famous of Wordsworth's early lyrics are those known as the *Lucy* poems. In them, we see for the first time certain qualities that were to become more and more common in Wordsworth's later poems. The most noticeable of these qualities is a new tone of tender personal emotion, at its best pure and strong, and at its worst dangerously near sentimentality. It is a quite different emotion from the sense of social, human sympathy with the general lot of men which underlies poems like *The Idiot Boy*, the *Female Vagrant*, the *Last of the Flock* and so on. With this new tone comes a whole new set of images and references, dealing with flowers, birds, stars and the smaller, prettier details of nature. The *Lucy* poems are not 'nature poems', as some of his later poems are nature poems, but they do point the way towards later works like *The Daisy*, *The Celandine*, *The Cuckoo* and *The Daffodils*.

Critics have spent much time discussing Lucy, and whether she was a real person, and if so, who. It is a fascinating problem, and one that is bound to arouse a certain amount of curiosity. From the poems themselves, it would seem that Lucy was an English girl whom Wordsworth loved, who lived in the Lake District, and who died at an early age; but the facts of Wordsworth's life do not bear this out. Nobody has ever been able to discover any satisfactory evidence of a girl known to Wordsworth who died young. There are certain vague and interesting hints of an adolescent affair at the age of seventeen, but they are very vague, and anyway there is no reason why, more than ten

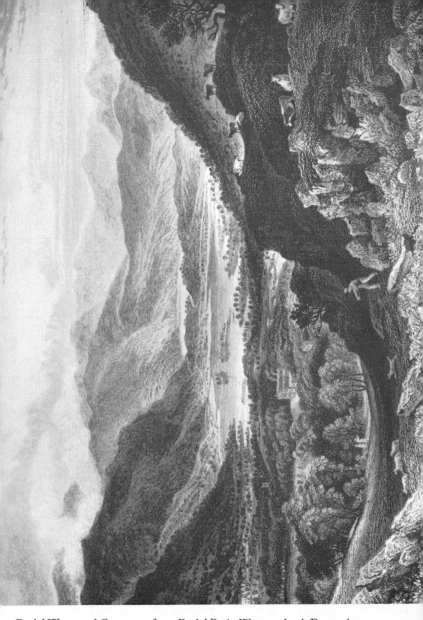

Rydal Water and Grasmere, from Rydal Park, Westmorland. Drawn by
G. Pickering, engraved by W. J. Cooke and published in 1835

William Wordsworth at the age of thirty-seven, drawn by
Sir Francis Legatt Chantrey

years later, and after a real love affair with Annette Vallon, he should suddenly remember and start to write poems about this long dead love. The poems are far more closely connected in many ways with the identity of his sister Dorothy, who is quite certainly the subject of one of them (*Strange Fits of Passion*), and so possibly of all. Dorothy, however, did not die, so why the girl Lucy should die in nearly all the *Lucy* poems remains something of a psychological mystery.

The poems were certainly written at a time when his relationship with Dorothy was at its most intense. Most of them were composed while he was abroad with her in Germany, during the bitterly cold winter of 1799; there, cut off from all other English companionship, unable to speak German, and undisturbed by any outside influences, he and Dorothy may well have spent much time recalling their early childhood, and dwelling intensely on the past. It was there too that Wordsworth started on his other great work about his childhood, *The Prelude*. Whatever Lucy's identity in real life, if she has one, it is quite clear that this group of poems shows the beginning of the profound influence that Dorothy had upon her brother, an influence that he acknowledged openly in verse time and time again; and indeed, from now on, they were never again to be separated, but spent the rest of their lives together.

In the lyric, *I travelled among unknown men*, Wordsworth almost seems to be telling, though indirectly, the story of his stay in Germany with Dorothy; in it, he tells how he did not fully realize the depths of his passion for Lucy and the country she lived in until he left England. He says this with the utmost simplicity, and on one level the statement seems so slight that it is hardly worth making—and yet at the same time one feels some powerful, elusive pressure behind it, some heartfelt inner meaning that gives the poem its haunting quality. The words that the poem uses are just as clear and simple as those in the ballad stories, but unlike the ballad words they are large and vague, and much less aggressively matter-of-fact; instead of saying that he went to Germany, he says:

E

> I travelled among unknown men
> In lands across the sea . . .

—and he describes his stay in this foreign country as 'a melancholy dream'. It was among the mountains of England, he says, that he first felt 'the joy of his desire', and this phrase is entirely typical of the poem; it *seems* perfectly straightforward, but the closer one looks at it, the less sure one becomes of its exact meaning. Is he speaking of desire for Lucy? Or desire for the mountains? And if he first felt the *joy* of his desire amongst English mountains, did he feel some other kind of desire somewhere else? The poem ends with another apparently simple statement; the poet says that England was the last country Lucy looked upon:

> And thine too is the last green field
> That Lucy's eyes surveyed.

This remark, too, is deceptive in its simplicity; it could possibly mean that Lucy is dead, and that she does not now survey any green fields at all—or it could merely mean that the last time Lucy looked at a field, it was, since she lives in England, an English one. The first of these meanings seems to be too big for the words, the second too little—the real meaning seems to lie, impossibly enough from a logical viewpoint, somewhere between the two.

Whatever the poem means (and it is clearly, unlike *The Idiot Boy*, almost impossible to paraphrase or turn into everyday prose), the effect of it is to bring together, in some curiously indirect way, the country and the girl, England and Lucy. England, to the poet, *is* Lucy; to him at least the two things mean the same. In missing one, he misses the other; in discovering the depth of his love for one, he discovers the depth of his love for the other.

The other *Lucy* poems have something of the same quality. Even the ballad *Lucy Gray*, a poem slightly different from the other *Lucy* lyrics, is quite unlike the other ballad stories, although like them it tells a story rather than expresses the poet's own personal feelings. It too has an unearthly, unreal quality, as though in it the poet were trying to say something personal and complicated about himself, not something about a little girl called Lucy Gray; it also has, in the last verses, a touch of the supernatural, which as we have seen is quite foreign to the earlier ballads. Like the Lucy of the other poems, Lucy Gray died young:

> Yet some maintain that to this day
> She is a living child;
> That you may see sweet Lucy Gray
> Upon the lonesome wild.
>
> O'er rough and smooth she trips along,
> And never looks behind;
> And sings a solitary song
> That whistles in the wind.

LUCY GRAY, 57–64

In *She dwelt among the untrodden ways*, Wordsworth carries the identification of the girl and the country even further. In this poem, he says that Lucy *is* 'a violet by a mossy stone'; she *is* 'a star'. Again, there is the same sense of vagueness, and the same emphasis on things 'unknown'; in the other poem, Wordsworth travelled among 'unknown men', and here it is Lucy who dwells 'among the untrodden ways' and who 'lived unknown'. He tells us nothing practical, nothing factual about her at all. Even the 'springs of Dove' that she dwelled beside are not a real place, which is odd only when one remembers what a passion Wordsworth had for using real places and real place names, and for giving his stories a detailed physical setting. All he tells us about Lucy in this poem is that she lived unknown, and that she is now dead. *Three years she grew in sun and shower* is even further from any kind of factual account of Lucy; it is a fanciful description of the way Nature takes Lucy to herself, and creates her. In theory, as he says in his *Preface*, Wordsworth was against the use of abstract personification of things like the Spirit of Nature or the

67

Muse of Poetry, but in this poem he uses a very full personification of nature himself. In this poem too Lucy dies, and leaves the poet desolate, with the memory of:

> . . . what has been
> And never more will be

though the details of what has been between Wordsworth and Lucy are left very vague and dim.

Perhaps the finest, though, of all the *Lucy* lyrics, and also the shortest, is *A Slumber did my spirit seal*, which can be quoted in full. It is an extraordinary poem, both in what it says, and in what it does not say.

> A slumber did my spirit seal;
> I had no human fears:
> She seemed a thing that could not feel
> The touch of earthly years.
>
> No motion has she now, no force;
> She neither hears nor sees;
> Rolled round in earth's diurnal course,
> With rocks, and stones, and trees.

In this poem the girl—Lucy, Dorothy, whoever it is—has reached the furthest point of disembodiment. She is not even a violet or a star; she is nothing as tangible or visible even as those two inhuman objects. The poem does not say that she has died; there is no factual statement of the kind. She is defined wholly by negatives; that is, we do not know who she was or what she was, only that she is no longer. She is nothing; she sees nothing, she hears nothing, she cannot herself move, she is beyond time, unchangeable, eternal. And yet, at the same time, she does move; she is not motionless, she moves with the movement of the whole world, as it turns in space, and this movement she almost seems to feel—certainly the poet feels it for her. The poem does not even say that she is in her grave, though this is what one tends to assume. Perhaps she, like the poet, is in a trance. For he too is in 'a slumber', carried beyond ordinary 'human fears'; he has no regrets, no anxieties, and he feels himself turning slowly, as though he has lost his own strength and his own right to action, as though he has become a rock or a stone or a tree.

And yet, at the same time, we do not feel that this trance is like death. We do not feel that the poet and Lucy are as dead as stones; the effect of the poem is to make us feel that stones and trees are alive, and that the daily turning of the earth is a positive, living movement, not a mere mechanical rotation. This highly complex notion, characteristic of Wordsworth's attitude to the natural world, is expressed in these two short verses with an amazing power and with a complete absence of any philosophical or intellectual argument: the poem has perfect unity. Every word in it is extremely simple and indeed common, with one interesting exception—'diurnal'—which is the only word in the poem with more than two syllables, and the only word that anyone might have to look up in a dictionary. It is the only literary word in the piece, and it is used with great care and effect. The heavy rolling of its syllables suggest the rolling of the earth, as the more usual word 'daily' could never have done, and its very unexpectedness adds immeasurably to the weight and gravity of the poem. Wordsworth does not overdo it; a poem full of words like 'diurnal' would be merely pedantic and artificial, but the use of one such word, accompanied by the bare dignity of 'rocks and stones and trees', is extraordinarily musical and suggestive. In his sparing, careful use of such long and rhythmic words, Wordsworth at his best is with Shakespeare. The combination of sound and sense is a sign of the greatest poetry.

As a footnote to the above poem, it is perhaps worth noting that both William and Dorothy used to think of death as of lying awake in the grave, and that they discussed this idea. In Dorothy's *Journal*, she writes:

> We went to John's grave, sate a while at first. Afterwards William lay, and I lay, in the trench under the fence—he with

his eyes shut, and listening to the waterfalls and the birds . . .
we both lay still, and unseen by one another; he thought that
it would be as sweet thus to lie so in the grave, to hear the
peaceful sounds of the earth . . .

(April 29, 1802)

This is an interesting sidelight on the poem, and on the closeness of Dorothy and William. Wordsworth as a child had found
it as hard as the little girl in *We Are Seven* to imagine the
finality of death, and in the *Ode on the Intimations of Immortality*
he writes that to the child the grave:

Is but a lonely bed without the sense or sight
Of day or the warm light,
A place of thought where we in waiting lie . . .

Coleridge found this whole idea so 'frightful' that on his
persuasion Wordsworth cut these lines from the *Ode*, and most
people would probably agree that it is a gloomy, morbid and
frightful idea, but it was not so to William or to Dorothy. To
them, with their sense of the livingness of the very earth and
stones, the thought of lying still like a stone in the ground was
not at all alarming.

WORDSWORTH'S BLANK VERSE

So far we have looked at examples of Wordsworth's ballads and
lyrics, both of which are to be found in the 1800 edition of the
Lyrical Ballads. After writing these poems, his imagination
could have developed in one of several ways; he was only thirty
when the 1800 edition came out, and at the start of the most
productive few years of his life. He could have concentrated on
writing narrative poetry in a ballad form, aimed at a fairly wide
popular audience. He could have become a lyric poet, writing
poems of personal feeling, with a more conventionally 'poetic'
subject matter. Or he could have made, as he did, a new departure. In the *Lyrical Ballads* there are some hints of this new
departure, which was to grow and to develop into his greatest
and longest work, *The Prelude*. This third kind of poetry is

different in form from both lyrics and ballads; it is in blank verse. This may at first sight seem a trivial difference, and certainly the metre of a poem is at best only a clue to its meaning, but nevertheless it is a very important clue. Wordsworth did not abandon the use of rhyme after the *Lyrical Ballads*, and the greatest part of his most popular nature poetry is in rhyming verse, but he was to develop blank verse into a peculiarly personal possession. In the *Lyrical Ballads* he uses blank verse in several of the narrative poems, like *Michael* and *The Brothers*, where the story, though homely enough, is too sober and sad for the bouncing metre of *The Idiot Boy*, and he also uses it in thoughtful pieces like *The Old Cumberland Beggar*. In these poems, however, the blank verse is conventional enough; it is only in pieces like *There was a Boy*, later to become part of *The Prelude*, that we find his own peculiar idiosyncratic blank verse style, a style that is quite different from his other manner. By 1800 he had only just begun to develop this new style, and there is not much of it in the *Lyrical Ballads*; perhaps the most striking and significant piece of it is the famous poem, *Lines composed a few miles above Tintern Abbey*.

Tintern Abbey, of all the other poems written at this date, is the one that points forward most clearly to *The Prelude*. Like the *Lucy* lyrics, it is personal in feeling, but unlike them it is quite openly and specifically so, and says exactly what and whom it is being personal about. Instead of addressing an unknown maid named Lucy, it addresses 'my dear, dear sister'. It is quite unlike both lyrics and ballads in style, for its language is not simple by any standards; both its grammar and its vocabulary are very complicated and sometimes obscure. In it, we see for the first time what is often labelled the 'Miltonic' side of Wordsworth—the long, involved sentences, the lofty emotions, the grand manner. (The long sentences, as a matter of fact, owe as much to Coleridge who was addicted to them, even in ordinary conversation, as to Milton.) And it is in *Tintern Abbey* that we see for the first time Wordsworth as 'a worshipper of nature'. It is not the first poem to show his sense of the importance of natural surroundings—other poems show his first-hand knowledge of country life, with its beauties and hardships. But it is *Tintern Abbey* that shows for the first time his romantic passion for nature, and in which he gives us highly emotional descriptions of the effects of the outer world upon his own inner self; this is the first poem in which he used, with deep feeling, phrases like 'a worshipper of nature', and speaks of 'the deeper zeal of holier love' that he feels for nature. The whole poem is a complicated, passionate outpouring, quite different in feeling from the narrative poems, and from the almost trance-like clarity of the *Lucy* lyrics. It is not really one of the lyrical ballads at all.

Perhaps the way in which it most closely resembles *The Prelude* is in its close connection with real events and emotions in the poet's own life. Indeed, it is hardly possible to understand it without knowing where, when, to whom and about what he wrote it, for these personal details are not only a part of the poem, they are what the poem is about. It does not stand without them. We could read *Michael* or *The Idiot Boy* or *She dwelt among the untrodden ways* without knowing anything about Wordsworth at all—though we understand them better with some knowledge—but we cannot read *Tintern Abbey* in the same way; to understand it at all, we have to pay attention to Wordsworth, and to his feelings for his sister Dorothy. It is the poet himself who invites this attention. He starts off by telling us of the occasion he is describing; he is revisiting Tintern Abbey, he says, which he last saw five years ago. The five years have been long ones, packed with change and, he implies, sorrows: they cover a crucial period of his life:

> Five years have past, five summers, with the length
> Of five long winters! and again I hear
> These waters, rolling from their mountain-springs
> With a soft inland murmur . . .

1–4

He follows this introduction with a long description of the

scene, but this description is completely different in kind from the conventional 'portraits of nature' that he draws in his earliest works like *An Evening Walk* and *Descriptive Sketches*. The emphasis is no longer on the scene itself, but wholly upon what the scene means to Wordsworth—upon what it meant to him five years ago, when he was twenty-three, and on what it means to him now, in 1798. He writes from an entirely personal angle. Almost every sentence begins with the word 'I'; he says: 'once again do I behold . . .', 'I again repose . . .', 'once again I see . . .', 'I have owed to them . . .', 'how oft in spirit have I turned to thee, O sylvan Wye . . .' In short, it is the value and the meaning of the scene that he is trying to describe, not its outward appearance, not how many trees there were in the woods, or the colour of the sky, or the noise of the river. He is painting a picture not of a landscape with river and trees, but of something much more complicated; he is trying to describe the inner workings of his own mind.

What he has to tell us of the workings of his mind is neither simple nor easy to understand; his attitudes towards nature and its influences on man are extremely complicated, and have been long and laboriously discussed from every possible standpoint. Critics have seen in his poetry all kinds of religious and philosophical beliefs, and have argued fiercely about whether he is a Pantheist or a Platonist, a Christian nature mystic or an atheist or a follower of Hartley or a follower of Godwin or a follower of Rousseau. The truth is that he is a little bit of all these things, and he certainly does not hold and stick to any one rigid code or system of belief; his many beliefs cannot possibly be reduced to any one simple message, or even to any one complicated message. It might be worth trying to list some of the many, various, and not wholly consistent attitudes towards nature that can be found in this one poem; such a list will at least give some impression of the mixed contents of his mind. In this poem, we see:

1. Nature as Comforter. (In absence, in sorrow, in the ugly rush of city life; see poems like *The Daffodils*.)

2. Nature as a doorway into a state of visionary trance-like insight. (The state in which, while contemplating nature, we 'are laid asleep in body, and become a living soul': a state of 'wise passiveness'.)

3. Nature as the object of appetite, as the object of a passion for the picturesque; the nature of the ardent sightseer. (As nature was to Wordsworth in 1793, and when he went on his tour of the Alps.)

4. Nature as a source of and scene for animal pleasures, such as skating, riding, fishing, walking.

5. Nature as the home of the spirit of the world, or as the physical embodiment of God himself.

6. Nature as the union or meeting point of the inner and outer worlds. (The eye and ear both perceive and create what they sense, Wordsworth says; one of his most difficult concepts is his idea that the boundary between the outer world of nature and the inner world of the mind is a shifting boundary, not a fixed one.)

7. Nature as the source of and guide to human morality. (Compare with episodes from *The Prelude* about the stolen boat and the birds stolen from snares.)

8. Nature as a source of simple joy and pleasure.

All these different attitudes to nature occur in the poem, in roughly the order that I have given them; then, in the last twenty lines, the poem goes back to its beginning, and comes full circle, for it ends with notion (1), the idea of nature as a comforter. He ends by telling his sister that, in times to come:

> if solitude, or fear, or pain, or grief,
> Should be thy portion, with what healing thoughts
> Of tender joy wilt thou remember me
> And these my exhortations. . . .   142–5

74

Nature is called upon to comfort his sister in the sorrows of life that she may in the future be called upon to endure; this was not to be a mere pious wish, for poor Dorothy was to have more than her fair share of pain and grief, and spent over twenty years in a wheelchair, ill in body and mind, and in those years nature was almost her only comfort.

Making a list of Wordsworth's attitudes in this way does no more, of course, than show how difficult it is to turn his views into a clear system or philosophy. The categories overlap. Some of them are extremely simple—nearly everyone, for instance, uses the world of nature as a source of physical enjoyment, and as a source of beauty and comfort. Some of them, on the other hand, are extremely abstruse, and quite impossible to put into simple terms; they are moreover very peculiarly his own, and very few people would agree with all his varying ideas. Indeed, he does not agree with all his own ideas all the time: his views changed as his moods and experiences changed.

There is no time to do more than note, in this brief account, some of the other most striking ways in which *Tintern Abbey* departs from the style of the other *Lyrical Ballads*. We have looked at its personal, biographical subject matter and its complicated philosophical approach. There remains the question of language. The language of this poem, whatever it is, is not the language of 'the middle and lower classes of society'. Words like 'elevated', 'sublime', 'interfused', 'genial', 'ecstasy' and 'zeal' are certainly not to be heard daily on the lips of any Cumberland shepherd. The syntax, too, is as far removed from ordinary conversation as the actual words; a look at the lines quoted from *Tintern Abbey* on page 48 will show the difference. And this sentence, compared with several others, and with a good deal of *The Prelude*, is relatively straightforward; if one stops to read it with care, one can at least be sure of the subject and verb and object, whereas some of Wordsworth's sentences cannot be unravelled at all. Clearly, when he wrote *Tintern Abbey*, Wordsworth was aiming at something quite unlike the aims fulfilled in a poem like *Michael* or *The Idiot Boy*. It does not follow from this, however, that because *Tintern Abbey* is good, all the other poems must be bad, and that the aims expressed in the *Preface* must be mistaken. The other poems are good, and in some ways they are more completely successful than *Tintern Abbey*, which hast its weak moments (what, for instance, are hermits—those Gothic trappings—doing in line 21?) and which points forward not only to the grand achievement of *The Prelude*, but also to some of the worst psuedo-poetic sublimities of Wordsworth's middle and old age. *Tintern Abbey* is not good at the expense of other poems in the book; it is good in quite a different way.

4

The Prelude

It is very difficult to know where to place *The Prelude*. Words-worth began to write it as early as 1799, and certain passages from it, such as *There was a Boy* and *Nutting*, were originally published along with the *Lyrical Ballads*, although they are as different from most of the poems of this period as *Tintern Abbey* itself. Most of the rest of this long work was composed over the years 1800–1805, though there were long gaps during this time when Wordsworth hardly looked at it. He had finished one version of it by 1805, but it was not published until after his death in 1850, and during the last forty-five years of his life he was continually altering, revising and adding to his original version. So the various texts of the poem cover a very long period in the poet's life, during which his style and his opinions both changed enormously. Luckily, there are good records of the dates at which changes were made, so that anyone interested in unravelling the development of the poem can do so; usually, however, the earlier version is the better and the more interesting. Later alterations do smooth out some of the clumsinesses of the 1805 text, but they also smooth out some of Wordsworth's most challenging and original ideas. When discussing *The Prelude*, it is always as well to be sure exactly which *Prelude* one is talking about: the different versions are printed side by side, with dates, in Ernest de Selincourt's edition of the poem (Oxford 1926), where they can be quickly and easily compared.

An added complication is the fact that the poem deals with Wordsworth's own early life and childhood. It was all written *after* 1798, when the *Lyrical Ballads* came out, but it is about the years *before* 1798. So what we have is a thirty-year old man starting to write about himself as a boy and as a young man, writing during one of the most changeful patches of his own life and continually retouching after the age of thirty-five. Not surprisingly, the poem is full of inconsistencies. Over such a time-span his attitude towards everything, not least towards the rights and wrongs of his own younger self, was bound to change considerably. It is not like a diary, written at the time and on the spot. The style in which he writes *The Prelude* is quite different from the style in which he would have written if he had been writing as a diary; the style is all post-*Lyrical Ballads*, the subject matter all pre-*Lyrical Ballads*.

NOT AN AUTOBIOGRAPHY

It is necessary to try to draw this distinction, difficult and clumsy as it is, because the same problems always arise when one tries to explain or interpret *The Prelude*. It is so closely concerned with Wordsworth's own life that it becomes very hard to decide whether one is talking about Wordsworth as a man, or Wordsworth as the writer of a piece of poetry describing a man called Wordsworth. There is also the problem of how seriously one takes the facts in the poem. Naturally enough, endless work has been done by critics, biographers and mere enthusiasts in trying to separate facts from fancy; reams of paper have been covered in discussions of which city Wordsworth means in line 7 of the Introduction, which town he was returning from in Book Four, which lake he sailed on in the stolen boat in Book One. Whole books have been devoted to whether or not his picture of life in Cambridge is a fair one, and churchyards and church registers have been scrutinized to find the identity of the boy who was so good at hooting at the owls. And the story of Annette Vallon, his French mistress, is the centre of a special detective-investigation of its own, though the truth is that in the whole of *The Prelude* Wordsworth does not even mention her: the story of Vaudracour and Julia has been commonly taken to be a discreet and veiled account of his own affair, and critics have gone through it with a toothcomb, seizing on this word and that as evidence of this or that theory, all the more stimulated by the almost total lack of evidence. This kind of curiosity is entirely natural, and Wordsworth does ask for it; it would not be possible to read *The Prelude* without wondering why on earth Vaudracour and Julia suddenly crop up in it, or why Wordsworth does not make any more direct mention of Annette Vallon.

Nevertheless, although one cannot help wondering about these things, they are not really what the poem is about. Perhaps the first most important point to get straight about *The Prelude* is to decide what it is *not*. It is not a simple account of the poet's life. Wordsworth never says that it is; he never claims to have got his facts right, or his dates right, or to have told the whole truth. Although it is a fascinating source of information, it was not written as information; it is no more an autobiography, in the usual sense, than *Tintern Abbey* is a description of an abbey. Its sub-title—'The Growth of a Poet's Mind'—shows that Wordsworth was not interested merely in facts. More than any of his other works, it was written to please himself; it is the most private of his poems. It was not written with any particular public in view, unlike the *Lyrical Ballads*, which, as we have seen, was deliberately calculated to make certain impressions on critics and readers. *The Prelude* was not even written for publication.

In form and structure, it is a peculiar and individual work. Like *Tintern Abbey*, it is in blank verse, and at times a very lofty blank verse; and like *Tintern Abbey*, it is addressed largely to one particular reader, this time not to his sister but to his greatest friend, Coleridge, with whom he had just produced the *Lyrical Ballads*. At times it resembles an epistle, or verse-letter, a form of poem popular in the eighteenth century, and much used by Pope. However, it is far longer than the usual epistle, and at times Wordsworth seems to forget Coleridge's existence entirely, and to write entirely for himself or for the general reader. In other ways it resembles an epic. It has noticeable similarities to

79

the most famous of English epics, *Paradise Lost*; it has the same metre, the same dignity and seriousness, and even in places the same highly involved sentence structure. And, like an epic, it is divided into Books. Wordsworth obviously had classical models in mind when constructing the poem, but typically enough his poem has thirteen Books, not the conventional twelve of *Paradise Lost* or the *Aeneid*. It differs from the true epic, too, in that it has no real story; an epic deals with actions, events, incidents, usually heroic or mythical, and the so-called cinema epics of today, films like *Ben Hur* and *Lawrence of Arabia*, are perfectly faithful to the epic tradition in their subject matter at least, for like Homer and Milton they are concerned with heroes and battles, death and suffering. *The Prelude* has no hero, and it is not directly concerned with outward events, though they play their part; its action takes place not in the outside world but in the poet's mind.

As a form, as a type of poem, *The Prelude* stands alone in English poetry. There is nothing quite like it. In some ways, particularly in its imaginative use of little details and incidents, outwardly trivial but inwardly full of meaning, it is more like a modern psychological novel than a poem. Although it is full of passages as lofty and powerful as anything in Milton, it is not a very delicately constructed or elegant work: there are thirteen books, not twelve, just because it happened to work out that way, not because it was planned that way. The style plunges from the extremely elevated to the everyday and prosaic, and then soars as unexpectedly up again. It has an odd lack of smoothness at times; it is hard to imagine any other poet capable of remarking, quite casually as Wordsworth remarks in Book Five:

> My drift hath scarcely,
> I fear, been obvious.   5, 291

—without even an apology, or an attempt to make the drift more obvious. This clumsy admission, despite constant revisions, was never smoothed away, and at this point in the poem it is quite true that Wordsworth's argument *is* hard to follow—so

William Wordsworth at seventy-two. Oil painting by B. R. Haydon

Springtime at Rydal Water, in the Lake District

hard that the next fifty lines or so, which are intended to paint a picture of the worst kind of education for a boy, have sometimes been taken as a description of Wordsworth's ideal child. The mistake is the reader's, but it is not an unnatural one, and not entirely the reader's fault.

In a way, though, these occasional faults of clumsiness and awkwardness add up to a kind of honesty. While reading the poem, one has very much a sense of following a truthful mind, which is all the more truthful for admitting to its confusions. Wordsworth, despite all his rewritings, was never a very polished poet; he preferred truth, however knotty and odd, to a smooth and pretty simplification, and when he could express himself only through the clumsy and the obscure he did not worry too much about being elegant. Some of the things he is trying to describe in *The Prelude* were indeed very difficult to put into poetry, and had never been dealt with in verse before. He was perfectly capable, as a poet, of lucid simplicity, as he shows in his lyrics, but in *The Prelude* he is tackling a much more complicated and confusing subject. He is the first poet to try to examine the human mind from a psychological viewpoint. What he tries to describe, as his sub-title to the poem suggests, is the working of the subconscious mind.

The word 'subconscious' is of course one that Wordsworth himself would never have used. Its first recorded use in the English language took place in 1832, long after *The Prelude* was written, and it did not become common until much later. Nowadays, in an age of psychologists and psychiatrists, everyone talks glibly about the subconscious, and most of us have at least a rough idea of what we mean when we use a phrase like 'subconscious desires', although hardly any of us could attempt to describe what Freud and Jung have said about them. The details of psychiatry are still a total mystery to most people, but the vague outlines of Freud's theories are now fairly well known; they are in the dim background of everyone's mind. In Wordsworth's day, however, this was not so; he was very much on his own.

At various points in *The Prelude*, he seems to be putting forward his own theory of the subconscious mind; there are many passages in which he describes the way that certain events, although unrecognized at the time, connect and link themselves together and gradually build up into a man's inner self. These events—they may not even be events, they may be merely feelings, or sights, or impressions—are but dimly perceived when they take place, but their influence is lasting. Wordsworth is quite clear about the tremendous significance of childhood experience and surroundings, a point on which any modern psychologist would agree with him, but the value of his ideas lies not so much in the ideas themselves as in the extraordinary detail and sensitivity with which they are expressed. He traces the details of the mind with extreme care; he holds a microscope over the small, almost invisible links that build up into principles, morals, actions, character. He does not give us just theories; he tries to show us the mind at work. He has an amazing gift for grasping the significance of the apparently insignificant, and for seeing all things as part of a meaningful whole; he tries to show us what he and his poetry are made of, and they are not made only of great events and emotions, of marriage and passion and the French Revolution, but of small things that a less observant or retentive mind would have forgotten—of boating expeditions, of chance meetings with old soldiers, of dreams, of the noise of the wind in the mountains, of the sight of the ash tree outside his bedroom window. These small, apparently disconnected events and impressions are to Wordsworth neither small nor disconnected. In *The Prelude* we see him tracing the links, joining them together, working out their meanings and what they have done to him. It is not surprising, in view of the complications and originality of this undertaking, that his drift is at times scarcely obvious, but even when we cannot quite follow his links, we feel that they are there, even if he has not quite managed to bring them up from the subconscious level into the light of day.

Wordsworth's notion of the subconscious is not in fact wholly original; it has certain connections with the ideas of the eighteenth-century philosopher Hartley (1705–57), who believed that our moral character is not born with us, but develops during childhood and youth, as a direct result of our physical experiences and the pleasure and pain they cause. This belief obviously places great stress on early background and environment, as does Wordsworth: Coleridge too was strongly influenced by Hartley, and in several of his poems he expresses his wish that his own child (named Hartley, incidentally, after the philosopher) should be brought up in close contact with the beautiful sights of nature, not with the ugliness of city life. In *The Nightingale*, for instance, published in the 1798 edition of the *Lyrical Ballads*, he describes the way in which one night his child awoke in tears; Coleridge took him out into the garden, and the sight of the moon hushed him and made him smile. He says that he hopes his child will grow up familiar with the songs of the nightingale, 'that with the night he may associate joy' (*The Nightingale*, line 107). This sense of the formative importance of environment can be found throughout *The Prelude*, but Wordsworth's attitudes to it are far less mechanical and more subtle than Hartley's, for he does not believe that man is nothing more than the result of his experiences; there is nothing rational or mechanical about his views of the mind's workings. He does not see things simply in terms of cause and effect, as Hartley tended to do; his views of the interconnections of events are far more complex, far nearer our modern psychological theories than the cruder theories of the eighteenth century. It is this sense of complexity and hidden connections that plays such havoc with the chronology of *The Prelude*.

So, when looking at *The Prelude*, what we must be careful *not* to look for is a straightforward autobiography, relating external events in an orderly fashion. As an autobiography, it is neither methodical nor complete. Instead of pursuing a straight course, from birth through childhood to adolescence and manhood, it meanders backwards and forwards. Wordsworth himself often compares his course in the poem to the course of the river; for instance, the whole of Book Eight, which is called Retrospect, is a recap or flashback which covers old ground instead of advancing the story, and Wordsworth opens Book Nine with a kind of apology for or explanation of his long detour:

> As oftentimes a River, it might seem,
> Yielding in part to old remembrances,
> Part swayed by fear to tread an onward road
> That leads direct to the devouring sea,
> Turns, and will measure back his course, far back,
> Towards the very regions which he crossed
> In his first outset; so have we long time
> Made motions retrograde, in like pursuit
> Detained. But now we start afresh; I feel
> An impulse to precipitate my Verse. . . .
>
> 9, 1–10

And at another point he apologizes for the opposite fault—that of getting unmethodically ahead of himself in his story—by saying that:

> I was hurried onwards by a stream
> And could not stop.
>
> 5, 183–4

There are many other similar references, in which he speaks of tracing his feelings back to their 'source', and he uses imagery drawn from rivers, lakes, inland waters, seas, brooks, and rills throughout the poem. There is one beautiful simile, in which he compares the way he examines his own past, part seeing and part imagining what he sees, to the way a man can gaze into water and see things in the depths of the water that are not really there:

> As one who hangs down-bending from the side
> Of a slow-moving Boat, upon the breast
> Of a still water, solacing himself
> With such discoveries as his eye can make,

84

Beneath him, in the bottom of the deeps,
Sees many beauteous sights, weeds, fishes, flowers,
Grots, pebbles, roots of trees, and fancies more;
Yet often is perplexed, and cannot part
The shadow from the substance, rocks and sky,
Mountains and clouds, from that which is indeed
The region, and the things which there abide
In their true dwelling; now is crossed by gleam
Of his own image, by a sunbeam now,
And motions that are sent he knows not whence,
Impediments that make his task more sweet;
—Such pleasant office have we long pursued,
Incumbent o'er the surface of past time . . .

4, 247–64

This long, almost epic simile describes most beautifully the inner workings of the mind, and its mysterious processes, without being at all dry or abstract, and without using any abstruse philosophical words; the suggestion that what we read into our past in memory is part reflection from the present, part pure accident, and part the image of our own later self, is made in the most imaginative and natural way. The picture of the man leaning out of the boat is carefully drawn, and works quite consistently on a real and on a psychological level; it describes the two things at once without artificiality or strain.

The whole course of the poem has this natural, unforced movement. It moves like a river, not like a man-made canal; it does not keep one goal in sight and proceed stubbornly towards it. Wordsworth waits for 'impulses' and 'creative breezes'; when he meets obstacles, he waits or turns aside or retreats a little to make a new start. His attitude is entirely non-mechanical, and such shape as the poem has is not imposed from outside, but springs naturally from the poet's own developing mind. He explores, he follows suggestions and possibilities, and at the beginning of the poem he has no real idea of where he will end up. It is a voyage of discovery, not a journey to a fixed destination.

In a book of this length, it would be useless to try to cover all the ground that *The Prelude* covers, so after this brief account of Wordsworth's method, perhaps the best thing would be to look at the three main chunks of experience that the poem recounts— his childhood, his adolescence, and his adventures in France. It must be remembered, however, that in the poem these subjects are not kept in any way separate, but are jumbled up together in the most disorderly fashion; Wordsworth skips from one period to another, from one subject to another, with no sense of time scheme at all. For instance, although he starts (albeit after a long introduction) in an orderly enough fashion in Book One, with his early childhood, he does not tell us one of the most important facts about that childhood—that he was an orphan—until Book Five, and we find references to the most primitive state of all, babyhood, not in Book One at all, but scattered throughout the other books more or less at random. So the reader's picture of what the child Wordsworth was really like is built up gradually, not acquired in a block. To emphasize this, it might be interesting to compare two passages taken from very different parts of the poem, but which deal with roughly the same years of his life: one the skating episode, from Book One, and the other from Book Eleven, where Wordsworth tells of his waiting for the horses on the moor just before his father's death.

These two passages illustrate the two influences which Wordsworth says affected his early years most strongly—the influences of beauty and fear. At the very beginning of his account of himself, he says:

> Fair seed-time had my soul, and I grew up
> Fostered alike by beauty and by fear   *1, 305–6*

—and one of his aims in examining his own past so closely is to discover exactly how and why these things marked him out for and turned him into a poet. All children must feel them both, to a certain extent, but Wordsworth was an extraordinarily impressionable child, and twenty years after an event he can remember it and relive it with a startling intensity. Here is his description of an evening's skating, an evening of pleasure and beauty, not fear—but it is worth remembering while reading it that it follows directly after, and is in deliberate contrast with the description of the evening of fear when he stole the boat, alone, and was so terrified by his experiences that for long afterwards:

> huge and mighty Forms that do not live
> Like living men moved slowly through my mind
> By day and were the trouble of my dreams . . .

1, 425–7

The skating episode has no such gloomy background; at first sight it is a simple account of an ordinary schoolboy's ordinary amusement:

> And in the frosty season, when the sun
> Was set, and visible for many a mile
> The cottage windows through the twilight blazed,
> I heeded not the summons:—happy time
> It was, indeed, for all of us; to me
> It was a time of rapture: clear and loud
> The village clock tolled six; I wheeled about,
> Proud and exulting, like an untired horse,
> That cares not for its home.—All shod with steel,
> We hissed along the polished ice, in games
> Confederate, imitative of the chase
> And woodland pleasures, the resounding horn,
> The Pack loud bellowing, and the hunted hare.
> So through the darkness and the cold we flew,
> And not a voice was idle; with the din,
> Meanwhile, the precipices rang aloud,
> The leafless trees, and every icy crag
> Tinkled like iron, while the distant hills
> Into the tumult sent an alien sound
> Of melancholy, not unnoticed, while the stars
> Eastward, were sparkling clear, and in the west
> The orange sky of evening died away.

1, 452–73

The most immediately impressive thing about this passage is of course its amazing vitality. It is a description of nature, in its way, but it could not be further from the languid, motionless still-life pictures drawn by eighteenth-century poets. It is full of noise and movement and colour; the frozen, icy countryside with its metallic hardness is beautifully described in words like 'steel', 'polished' and 'iron'; the glad animal noises of the shouting boys are contrasted with the larger, distant sound of the hills echoing with 'an alien sound of melancholy'; and then, at the end, the whole wintry scene is suddenly flooded and warmed by the wonderfully unexpected '*orange* sky of evening'. The episode is seen through the eyes of a participant, through the eyes of a boy who was there and part of the 'pack loud bellowing', and not through the eyes of a middle-aged spectator taking nature notes; the actual sensation of skating is as much a part of the poem as the attempt to describe the hills and stars and sunset. It is all felt, not merely seen as through a window, and we can sense the boy's tremendous excitement and skill; he really means it when he says: 'for me it was a time of rapture'—(even as an old man, incidentally, Wordsworth still had the reputation for being a great skater: he was said to be able to cut his name in the ice).

In the passage quoted, however, most of the sights and sensations would have been noticed by most of the boys out skating. Even the 'alien sound of melancholy' was 'not unnoticed'; it was part of the background of their excitement. The boy Wordsworth saw more clearly, and he remembered: so far that is the only difference between him and his school friends. It is in the following passage that we see him as someone special, as a poet in the making, set very slightly apart from his friends:

> Not seldom from the uproar I retired
> Into a silent bay, or sportively
> Glanced sideway, leaving the tumultuous throng,
> To cut across the image of a star
> That gleamed upon the ice: and oftentimes
> When we had given our bodies to the wind,

And all the shadowy banks, on either side,
Came sweeping through the darkness, spinning still
The rapid line of motion; then at once
Have I, reclining back upon my heels,
Stopped short, yet still the solitary Cliffs
Wheeled by me, even as if the earth had rolled
With visible motion her diurnal round;
Behind me did they stretch in solemn train
Feebler and feebler, and I stood and watched
Till all was tranquil as a dreamless sleep.

1, 474–89

Here we see Wordsworth deliberately setting himself apart, and seeking solitude, as he was to do much more often when older. On one level, what he does and what he sees are perfectly ordinary; the feeling of giddiness which he describes is common enough, and is felt by any child who spins round and round until it feels dizzy. The sense, after violent movement, that the earth is still going round and round is common, just as skating is a common pastime, available to everyone. It is the way in which Wordsworth describes it that shows what an important experience it was to him. It is the kind of experience that no other writer had taken seriously enough to write about; every writer who ever lived must have felt it, but Wordsworth was the first for whom it had significance, for whom it had a permanent meaning. It remained awake in his imagination; it was not one of those childish fancies that are soon forgotten.

It is hard to describe or to understand exactly what this experience did mean to him. On one level, he clearly sensed, even as a boy, the livingness of the world itself. To him the earth was not a dead cinder turning aimlessly in space, but a living, moving, feeling thing; at some moments, as in the quiet moments after skating, he felt aware of this mysterious life as other, religious men are aware of the presence of God. To him, the sense of the turning earth was not a mere trick of unbalanced ear drums, but a revelation of some profound truth about the nature of life itself. There *is* a simple physical explanation, just as there is a simple physical explanation of the way in which the dark peak appeared to follow the stolen boat—and Wordsworth is not fool enough to think that the peak really followed the boat, or that he really felt the world turn on its axis. But the explanation is different from the meaning. He was convinced that these sensations *meant* something to him: they were messages, revelations, warnings. This is how Wordsworth differs from the other boys; the other boys felt mere dizziness, but Wordsworth felt the turning world.

Indeed, in the very next line of the poem, Wordsworth moves on to an almost religious, exalted tone; using language which is positively Biblical, he says:

> Ye Presences of Nature, in the sky
> Or on the earth! Ye Visions of the hills!
> And Souls of lonely places! can I think
> A vulgar hope was yours when Ye employed
> Such ministry . . .
>
> *i*, 490-4

—and describes, in an enormously powerful image, how these presences made:

> . . . the surface of the universal earth
> With triumph, and delight, and hope, and fear,
> Work like a sea.
>
> *i*, 499-501

In other words, these mysterious sensations of his had singled him out, and set him apart from his friends in a 'hope' that he would become a poet; these feelings of his as a child were the beginnings of his poetic power. He believed that these presences were something outside himself, not something in his own heart; to him, the surface of the earth was seething with life and with emotion, just as he himself was. The earth was alive, and he was alive, and to him the boundaries between the two were not distinctly marked. We can explain his conviction by saying that he himself was so full of vitality that in his imagina-

90

tion he spread his sense of life over lifeless objects, or we can believe with him that the life and the power were truly there; it does not really matter which way we look at it. The important thing is to grasp that for him every object in the outside world was full of an inner life—the cliffs, the lakes, the mountains all spoke to him. He describes in Book Three the way in which he saw life and read feelings into the very stones of the road:

> To every natural form, rock, fruit or flower,
> Even the loose stones that cover the highway,
> I gave a moral life, I saw them feel . . .

3, 124–6

As a child, he was not of course fully aware of the peculiarity nor of the importance of these feelings; it was only years later that he could make sense of them, and interpret them, as he does in the philosophical passages of *The Prelude*, like the one just quoted, beginning 'Ye Presences of Nature'. But it is also true that if, as he grew older, he was better able to describe these feelings, he also experienced them more and more rarely. This is one of the reasons why he writes in such detail of his childhood, because it was during his childhood that his sense of communication with natural objects was at its most powerful. As a matter of fact, this sense of communication with objects can be seen in most young children, though often in a very elementary form: children do not draw nearly such hard and fast lines between things and people as adults do. They can invest teddy bears and rocking chairs and even old toothbrushes with human feelings and human life, and most children's stories are based on the notion that rabbits and hedgehogs can talk and think. I am not suggesting that Wordsworth indulged in this kind of crude childish fantasy; he was never a boy for fanciful chats with rabbits and butterflies. His imagination was far grander, more gloomy and severe; there was nothing pretty or comfortable about his sense of the earth's secret powers. But at the same time it is true that children are more likely to imagine things and see things in this way than adults are, even children with very little imagination at all; it is a faculty that fades with age, as Wordsworth discovered.

In this passage about skating, then, Wordsworth presents us with several things at once. First and most obviously, he shows us the scene itself, in vivid detail: all the physical aspects are described. We know the time, the place, the weather, who was there, what they were doing, everything; it is clear, precise and not in the least fanciful or romantic. Then he shows us himself as a boy, separate from the scene and yet part of it. And then he goes on to describe the 'presences of nature' that he felt on such occasions, that watched over him, and 'haunted him thus among his boyish sports'. So he gives us the scene, his place in it, and its meaning. Perhaps the most important thing to note is that the philosophical, reflective passage about the presence of nature does not stand on its own, but is closely linked to the mood of physical excitement. Wordsworth very rarely thinks in the abstract, with his head only; all the most visionary and mystical passages in *The Prelude* are directly linked to some ordinary physical event, like climbing Snowdon, crossing the Alps, or walking home after a dance. He may go beyond everyday life, but he always starts from it.

The second piece about his childhood, the piece about the waiting for the horses, is equally closely linked to a particular time and place, but in this case the time and the place are associated with memories of fear and sorrow, not with memories of beauty and enjoyment. The passage, too long to quote in full, begins (Book Eleven, line 346) with an account of how the boy Wordsworth, one Christmas time, goes to watch for the horses that are to take him home for the holidays the next day. He goes to watch from a high crag, where he has a good view of the two possible ways they might come; he is in an overwrought, 'feverish', end-of-term mood:

> 'Twas a day
> Stormy, and rough, and wild, and on the grass
> I sate, half-sheltered by a naked wall;

Upon my right hand was a single sheep,
A whistling hawthorn on my left, and there,
With those companions at my side, I watched . . .
      Ere I to School returned
That dreary time, ere I had been ten days
A dweller in my Father's House, he died,
And I and my two Brothers, Orphans then,
Followed his Body to the Grave. The event
With all the sorrow which it brought appeared
A chastisement; and when I called to mind
That day so lately passed, when from the crag
I looked in such anxiety of hope,
With trite reflections of morality,
Yet in the deepest passion, I bowed low
To God, who thus corrected my desires;
And afterwards, the wind and sleety rain
And all the business of the elements,
The single sheep, and the one blasted tree,
And the bleak music of that old stone wall . . .
All these were spectacles and sounds to which
I often would repair, and thence would drink,
As at a fountain; and I do not doubt
That in this later time, when storm and rain
Beat on my roof at midnight, or by day
When I am in the woods, unknown to me
The workings of my spirit thence are brought.

11, 356–89

Here again, as in the skating scene, we have the physical
details of the setting described with extreme clarity and vividness; the cold bleak dreariness is forcefully presented, but even
more forcefully presented is the powerful effect that it had on
the child's imagination. To him, the bleakness of the scene and
the death of his father are inseparably connected, and he even
looks on his father's death as a punishment for looking forward
too much to the Christmas holidays. It is a child's attitude; there
is no real logical connection between the dreary moor, the death
of Mr. Wordsworth, and the boy's end-of-term excitement. But
all these things remain so closely linked in his subconscious mind

that, even as a man, he still feels them to be part of the same experience. The link is subconscious, not conscious; a modern writer or poet would try to explain it in terms of psychology, but Wordsworth, without any of the language of psychology, makes a very good attempt to explain how the mind works; 'unknown to me', he says, even in later years 'the workings of my spirit' are roused by this distant knot of associations. His character, the pattern of his mind and the way it works, have been formed by these childhood experiences; the sound of rain on the roof reminds him as a man of what he felt as a child on that bare hillside. The childhood memory strengthens and refreshes him; he drinks from it 'as from a fountain'.

The process which he is trying to describe is a very complicated process; he was one of the first writers to try to put into words the mysteriousness of the workings of the spirit. Other writers had tried to deal with certain parts of this process; his contemporary Crabbe, for instance, in a curious poem called *The Lover's Journey*, describes the way in which a landscape can alter according to our own mood, and tells of how gay and bright everything seems to the lover as he rides to visit his mistress, and how dreary and gray the very same things seem as he rides disappointed home again. But Crabbe's poem, though good in its way, is very crude and mechanical when compared with the real insight of Wordsworth's attitude to nature. The idea that the experiences of the child affect the man is not of course wholly new, either—people have always known that upbringing and background have *some* effect—but Wordsworth was the first writer to appreciate many of the subtle implications of the idea. For him, everything that happens to a child happens to him with a purpose, and helps to form and teach him, and to make him grow; even the smallest, most accidental-seeming events and sights can join together into mighty influences. The apparently dead and careless world of nature is, as Wordsworth sees it, watching over the growing boy like a mother, ready to help, to inspire and to reprove; he is attached to the earth itself. Again and again during *The Prelude*, Wordsworth speaks of drinking and feeding from nature; he uses the image of the child feeding at the breast, he speaks of breasts and bosoms, he says that nature is his 'nurse' and 'fosters' him. When he examines his own past and childhood in *The Prelude*, one of his chief objects is to describe and to analyse this bond between himself and nature; he is conscious, as few are conscious, that he has been reared and watched over by everything about him, that every experience of the child, from evenings on the frozen lake to a lonely vigil with a sheep, has helped to form him into a man and a poet. As he himself so memorably said, 'the child is father of the man'—a remark which is, characteristically of Wordsworth, neither as simple nor as trite as it seems at first sight.

THE DEDICATED SPIRIT

As a child, Wordsworth felt he was being watched over and cared for, but he did not know why. From an early age, however, he seems to have had a sense that he was being singled out for some special purpose, and that nature was bestowing rather an unusual amount of time and trouble on him. People tend to take offence when he refers to himself as 'a favoured being', and to think it conceited of him to say so himself, even if it is true; but of course it is true, and to do him justice, Wordsworth never tries to take the credit for his own special blessedness himself. However one looks at it, he was a favoured being, if to be a great poet is to be favoured, and he became aware during his late teens that he was cut out to be a great poet. He could not help it; it just happened to him, and for the first half of his life at least he is very humble about it. In fact, at the beginning of *The Prelude*, he apologizes to Coleridge for talking so much about himself, and stresses the fact that he has not chosen himself as a subject through conceit, but through a genuine desire to straighten himself out. Also, he did not write for publication; his last intention was to impress the public with his own specially blessed importance.

He was, however, from the first a highly-gifted child, and as he grew older he gradually became aware of his special gift for poetry. The story of *The Prelude* is in part the story of this growing awareness, and of the responsibility he owes to his own talents—as he puts it, it is an account of 'the growth of a poet's mind'. As a child, he was not noticeably odd or peculiar; he was not an infant prodigy, like Mozart; he could not read Greek at the age of three, like John Stuart Mill; although a strongly imaginative child, his fancies were not all gloomy and morbid. He did well at school, but not alarmingly well, and when he went to Cambridge he had no interest in getting a brilliant degree. In fact, for so gifted a nature, his interests were as normal and sociable as could be expected; he confesses that he could only 'cleave to solitude in lonesome places', and that if there were friends around he could not keep away from them, for his heart 'was social, and loved idleness and joy'. A sense of dedication to poetry came over him only gradually, in odd moments of solitude; he was no moon-struck romantic, cut off from ordinary life.

In Book Four of *The Prelude*, *Summer Vacation*, he describes some of the moments during which he first became conscious of his own powers. One of them, which he tells in some detail, took place while he was walking home alone early one morning, after spending the whole night at a dance in a nearby village; when he starts to describe this walk, he seems to be criticizing himself for spending rather too much time at dances, and hardly any in 'thought and quietness'. Here is his description of his walk home:

> Ere we retired,
> The cock had crowed, the sky was bright with day.
> Two miles I had to walk along the fields
> Before I reached my home. Magnificent
> The morning was, a memorable pomp,
> More glorious than ever I beheld.
> The Sea was laughing at a distance; all
> The solid Mountains were as bright as clouds,
> Grain-tinctured, drenched in empyrean light . . .

Ah! need I say, dear Friend, that to the brim
My heart was full; I made no vows, but vows
Were then made for me; bond unknown to me
Was given, that I should be, else sinning greatly,
A dedicated Spirit. On I walked
In blessedness, which even yet remains.

4, 327–41

In this passage, Wordsworth is writing about a knot or lump
of associations, just as he does in the passage about his wait for
the horses. The sense of 'blessedness' which he speaks of in the
last line does not just descend on him suddenly, out of the blue;
it is very closely linked to what has gone before. The circumstances are all important. He had just spent the whole night
dancing, in a crowded, stuffy room, enjoying himself but feeling
a faint sense of guilt for doing so; then he had set off towards
home, finding himself suddenly alone, and no longer in the dark
but surrounded by all the beauty of an exceptionally sunny and
beautiful dawn. All these things—his gay evening, his guilt, his
sudden release into the fresh air, his sense of the startling beauty
of nature—join together into a feeling of blessedness and
responsibility; he feels suddenly full of power, and knows that he
must live up to himself, whatever he does. He does not say that
he is going to go off at once to start writing poetry—in fact he
does not even mention poetry at all—but he clearly has poetry in
mind when he speaks of the 'bond unknown to me'. Apart from
that, his idea of the bond is not very precise, and cannot be put
into words; the word 'unknown' must be used countless times in
The Prelude, just as it is in the *Lucy* lyrics.

It is interesting to note that nearly all of Wordsworth's most
significant experiences, as told in *The Prelude*, can be made to
sound simply ridiculous if put into other words. If one cuts out
all the vivid circumstantial detail that makes them so alive and
convincing, one is left with the silliest arguments, on this kind
of level: 'Because the river Derwent flowed past my house when
I was five years old, I ought to write good poetry, not bad
poetry (Book One, 270)'; 'Because I was so keen to get home

that I went to wait for the horses, my father died' (Book Eleven, 346); 'The morning when I walked home was so beautiful that something (not me) promised I should be an important poet one day' (as in the piece just quoted). This kind of paraphrase is completely meaningless when applied to Wordsworth, because he is not writing about rational experiences, which can be explained in logical argument; he is writing about the subconscious and the irrational. There is no *reason* why Wordsworth should have been born a poet, and not a mathematician or a shepherd; it is not his own doing, and this is why he feels that the bonds are made *for* him and not *by* him. When he says 'I felt a sense of dedication and vocation', he is not presenting an argument, any more than if he had said 'I love my mother', or 'I miss my family'. We do not believe Wordsworth because of the bare facts of what he says—after all, anyone is free to think he is a favoured being—but because he tells us so convincingly. He does not offer us an abstract, disembodied notion, but instead describes to us all circumstances in which he felt this sense of blessedness—the place, the time of day, the mood in which he was when he set off on his walk home. Even in this description, which has a loftier tone than some others ('grain-tinctured', 'empyrean', 'memorable pomp'), there is the freshness of real dawn; Wordsworth was not one of those poets who write rapturously about the beauty of the morning without ever getting up early enough to see it. What he says he has seen, he has seen, and what he says he has felt, he has really felt; the one helps to convince us of the other.

Incidentally, Wordsworth's description of himself as a young poet, wandering along composing poetry like 'a sick lover', offers a peculiarly characteristic mixture of the sublime and the ridiculous, of which he himself is quite aware—he says he used to wander along the road like an idiot, and when he hit on a particularly wonderful line, when:

> Some fair enchanting image in my mind
> Rose up, full-formed, like Venus from the sea.   *4*, 104–5

—what did he do but rush to share his excitement with his dog? The contrast between Venus and the rough little terrier, and the picture of the poetic young man sharing his ecstasy with a dog, is both touching and true and not quite ludicrous—there are not many poets willing to see themselves in this light, nor to tell others the homely details of their great moments of inspiration. Wordsworth is not anxious that his public should see him 'in his singing robes'; he is quite happy to show himself as a boy going for a walk with a dog.

THE FRENCH REVOLUTION

The last few books of *The Prelude* deal largely with the impact of Wordsworth's visit to France, and its lasting effects upon him. Until this point in the poem, most of the things he writes of are personal, concerned only with himself, and his own reactions; he tells us very little of the outside world, apart from a few brief impressions of Cambridge and London, and very little of his own friends and family. He is as deeply affected by mountains and lakes as by other people; in his account of his holiday in the Alps he hardly mentions his companion, Jones. Like most intelligent young people, he is self-absorbed, fascinated by the workings of his own mind, more interested in the effect things have on him than in the things themselves. He is highly introspective. From what he tells us of himself in these first books, it is very hard to imagine him as the author of the *Lyrical Ballads*, with their wide knowledge of human nature, their sympathy with human problems, and their complete lack of self-interested indulgence.

It is in the last five books of *The Prelude* that this change came about; it was caused by a great shock from outside, by the impact of the events of the outside world. It happened at just the right time; Wordsworth was in need of change. By the time he was twenty-one, his adolescent introspection was beginning to stagnate; he writes to a friend: 'I am doomed to be an idler through my whole life. I have read nothing this age, nor indeed did I ever . . .' It was natural enough that he should feel aimless

99

for, having finished his years at Cambridge, he simply did not know what to do next; he had no money, and the two careers open to him, teaching and the church, seemed dreary and unattractive. He had a sense of power and ability, but no outlet for it, and no way of earning his living by it. So he did what innumerable newly-made graduates and school-leavers in the same predicament still do today; he went abroad for a few months, to fill in time, and to escape from his family. But the world he escaped into was not the comparatively safe world known to hitch-hikers and *au pair* girls and wandering students today; it was the violent world of the French Revolution. France was in the grip of one of the most stormy, bloody social wars of history, and the sight of its struggles gave Wordsworth's unworldly, inward nature a shock which he was never to forget, and which altered the whole course of his life. And as if a war were not enough, it was on this same time-killing student's visit that he had his first and most passionate love affair, and became a lover and a father. If he went abroad with the idea of learning a little French, he certainly got more than he had bargained for; but if, as is more likely, he went because he felt a need to widen his vision, to achieve independence and maturity, then he could hardly have chosen better. He was to return to England a changed man.

When he set off for France, he knew very little about the world he was entering. His sympathies were on the whole with the Revolution, as were those of most liberal-minded young people in England, but he did not really know what was going on, except in the most general way. His sympathy did not go very deep; it was more a vague feeling of good will than a positive understanding and approval. On his way to Orleans, where he was intending to stay, he passed through Paris, where he saw the sights, as any sightseer would; he visited the ruins of the Bastille, which had fallen two years before, and pocketed a stone from it as a keepsake. But he admits, with his own peculiar honesty, that the sight of the Bastille did not stir his heart or imagination as it might have done; he says he—

> looked for something that I could not find,
> Affecting more emotion than I felt

9, 70–1

In other words, his reactions were dutiful, rather than spontaneous; he was like a tourist who admires the Venus de Milo not because he really likes it, but because he thinks he ought to like it. He compares his state as a visitor in Orleans to that of a greenhouse plant, carefully protected, safe and untouched:

> when every bush and tree, the country through,
> Is shaking to the roots . . .

9, 89–90

He was not hard-hearted, nor indifferent to what was going on around him; he just did not understand it. He was, in his own words, 'unprepared with needful knowledge'; he did not appreciate the issues at stake, nor the rights and wrongs of the war. He was a foreigner, and he felt as a foreigner.

He might have continued in his ignorance, and returned to England as well-meaning and uninformed as when he left it, had it not been for a chance encounter. While he was in Orleans, he met an officer named Beaupuis, stationed in the town; this man taught him the most important lessons of his life. All the other officers in the regiment were royalists, in sympathy with the old régime, but Beaupuis was for the people; he must have been a very remarkable man, to have seen through and stood out against all the pressures of his own aristocratic background and military surroundings. He and Wordsworth became close friends, and from him Wordsworth learned a feeling for humanity that he had never had before. He learned for the first time, through Beaupuis, to look on men as social beings, and to feel himself as part of society; he learned that poverty is an ill that can and must be put right, and that all men should be equal, and not separated by birth and wealth and privilege. It was here that he learned, in Pope's phrase, that 'the proper study of mankind is man'.

Beaupuis, although an exceptionally far-sighted and warm-hearted man, was no rash idealist; he had no illusions about the revolution, and did not see all working men as saints in disguise. He knew quite well that they were up against ignorance and poverty and uncontrolled violence, but he was tolerant and reasonable, and held fast to his principles. A better teacher could not have been found, and Wordsworth was at exactly the right age to learn; he was open, sensitive, easily moved, not selfish or withdrawn. He and Beaupuis would talk for hours of the evils of monarchy and the rights of the people, and some of their political discussions were doubtless radical and theoretical enough, but nevertheless they never strayed far from reality. For the reality was there, before their eyes; Beaupuis did not have to look far for his illustrations. In one brief episode, Wordsworth brings the whole mood of these conversations to life:

> And when we chanced
> One day to meet a hunger-bitten Girl,
> Who crept along, fitting her languid self
> Unto a Heifer's motion, by a cord
> Tied to her arm, and picking thus from the lane
> Its sustenance, while the Girl with her two hands
> Was busy knitting, in a heartless mood
> Of solitude, and at the sight my Friend
> In agitation said, "Tis against *that*
> Which we are fighting,' I with him believed
> Devoutly that a spirit was abroad
> Which could not be withstood, that poverty,
> At least like this, would in a little time
> Be found no more . . .

9, 510–23

Here, in this short passage, we see the depth of his new-found sympathy with man, and his new awareness of the hardships of the weak and poor; this poor French cow-girl, thin, hungry and listless, is one of the first of Wordsworth's pitiable victims of society. He had seen such sights before, in England;

he had seen beggars and disbanded soldiers enough, but he had not fully understood what he had seen. It was Beaupuis who explained to him the causes of hardships and poverty, and who showed him that they must be fought against and denounced. Beaupuis himself fought against poverty and inequality, and lost his life in battle; Wordsworth, being an Englishman and not a Frenchman in revolutionary France, wrote the *Lyrical Ballads*. But the spirit of battle was the same in both of them, and in their way the *Lyrical Ballads* are a blow in the cause of social justice. It is quite clear that Wordsworth owes his social conscience more to Beaupuis than to any revolutionary Godwinian tract; he does not mention Godwin anywhere in *The Prelude*, but he writes of Beaupuis with deep affection. The man's character meant as much to him as any abstract theory; there is something warm and real in his feelings for Beaupuis and the cow-girl, something quite different from the impractical extremist notions of many nineteenth-century radicals and politicians.

It is here, too, in the lesson that Wordsworth learned in France, that we find the real root of his theories about poetic diction. His impatience with empty, meaningless, flowery phrases springs from the same source as his disgust with the empty, vain, corrupt, aristocracy who could turn a blind sophisticated eye on starving girls and soldiers and soldiers' wives. Notice how the very language in which he describes the cow-girl acquires the stark dignity of the *Ballads*; the subject is powerful enough in itself, it needs no ornamental descriptions. In Wordsworth's view, one has only to look at such a sight to be moved. He is saying all the time in his poetry, "Tis against that which we are fighting'. His indignation is not artistic and aesthetic; it is human.

DISILLUSION AND COMFORT

The conclusion of *The Prelude* (Books Ten to Thirteen) tells the story of Wordsworth's return to England, of his bitter disillusion with the course of events in France, and of his struggles to find for himself a satisfying way of life. For him, this was a period of crisis and confusion, from which he emerged with great difficulty. Everything seemed to be against him. He was penniless, forced to return to England for lack of money, and still without any clear idea of how to earn his living. He left in France his mistress and newly-born daughter, and must have felt overwhelming guilt and anxiety on their behalf, though he says nothing about them in the poem. He also left in France all his political hopes and, when he returned to his own country, he found a very different attitude towards the French. The tide of feeling had turned against the revolutionaries, and England shortly declared war on France. To Wordsworth this was a bitter blow, and all the more bitter because he could see for himself that all was not well with the Revolution. Its noble aims were becoming obscured by bloodiness and violence; Robespierre was terrorizing the more liberal-minded leaders of the people, and meaningless atrocities like the September Massacres were common. To a young man who had written, in full hope and confidence:

> Bliss was it in that dawn to be alive,
> But to be young was very heaven

10, 693-4

—the course of events must have seemed like a personal betrayal. He had pinned his faith on the people, and the people were letting him down. His loyalties were horribly divided; he had no sympathy with the English, nor with the French royalists, but his sympathy with the people was already filled with doubts and misgivings. His new-found political consciousness was undergoing a hard trial.

He tells us of this trial in some detail, though his sequence of events is more than usually confused, probably because his hopes and fears were perpetually fluctuating; at one moment he hoped all might still turn out for the best, and at the next such optimism seemed a stupid illusion. He suffered all the more because he had expected so much. As he writes:

It was a lamentable time for man
Whether a hope had e'er been his or not,
A woeful time for them whose hopes did still
Outlast the shock; most woeful for those few,
They had the deepest feeling of the grief,
Who still were flattered, and had trust in man.

10, 356–61

For Wordsworth, the shock was not to his ideals and intellect only, but to his whole being; his despair was not intellectual, but made up in part of real physical terror, which we can understand only if we remember that he was actually in Paris during one of its most violent periods, and that he had seen with his own eyes sights that other Englishmen had only read about. He felt himself personally involved, threatened (as his mistress and child were still threatened) by real danger. He tells Coleridge:

Most melancholy at that time, O Friend!
Were my day-thoughts, my dreams were miserable;
Through months, through years, long after the last beat
Of those atrocities (I speak bare truth,
As if to thee alone in private talk)
I scarcely had one night of quiet sleep
Such ghastly visions had I of despair
And tyranny, and implements of death . . .

10, 369–76

This is not a description of a disappointed man, but of a man suffering from a nightmare. There is something peculiarly urgent and anxious in the odd, clumsy little parenthesis—'I speak bare truth, as if to thee alone in private talk', he says to Coleridge, as if trying to convince his friend that he is not exaggerating, that he is not being melodramatic about himself. He really was in a miserable and unbalanced state. If we remember this, it helps to account for his later change of heart, and to explain how he became so violently anti-French; in the second half of his life he was haunted, quite unreasonably, by the fear that England would have a revolution of its own, which might result in similar bloodshed and atrocities, and at the end, as a final crowning insult, bring England no more than another Napoleon.

He did not emerge from this state of nightmare without help. His account of how he regained confidence in himself, and of how his imagination was 'repaired and restored', is by no means clear; he did recover, and he did keep his faith in man, as the *Lyrical Ballads* show, but the exact stages of his recovery are hard to follow. What is clear, however, is the great debt that he owed to Coleridge and to his sister Dorothy. It was at this period that his life became closely bound up with theirs— indeed, it was at this time that he first met Coleridge, and he had never before been able to spend any time with Dorothy, owing to the early dispersal of the family. Now, thanks to a small and quite unexpected legacy, he and Dorothy were able to fulfil their dream of setting up house; Coleridge lived only a few miles away, and the three of them spent most of their time together. Here, in a passage from Book Ten of *The Prelude*, he describes the way that they gradually managed to console him, and helped him to recover from the disastrous after-effects of his adventures:

>   . . . Ah! then it was
> That Thou, most precious Friend! about this time
> First known to me, didst lend a living help
> To regulate my Soul, and then it was
> That the beloved Woman in whose sight
> Those days were passed, now speaking in a voice
> Of sudden admonition, like a brook
> That does but cross a lonely road, and now
> Seen, heard and felt, and caught at every turn,
> Companion never lost through many a league,
> Maintained for me a saving intercourse
> With my true self; for, though impaired and changed
> Much, as it seemed, I was no further changed
> Than as a clouded, not a waning moon:

She, in the midst of all, preserved me still
A Poet, made me seek beneath that name
My office upon earth. . . .

10, 905–21

This is only one of many tributes to Coleridge and Dorothy, and they were well-deserved. From his friendship with Coleridge sprang the *Lyrical Ballads*, which he began to write at this period, in one of the most successful examples of collaboration in literary history; the two men, though unlike in many ways, were passionately interested in the same things, shared the same radical political outlook, the same hatred of social injustice, the same highly critical and intelligent interest in the literature of the day. They encouraged and stimulated each other, and the great outburst of creative activity that covers these years shows that their debt, like their admiration, was mutual. The *Lyrical Ballads* are the direct result of the combined influence of Coleridge and the French Revolution; the latter supplied the ideals and the driving power, and the former supplied the 'regulation' necessary for turning the power into poetry.

Wordsworth's debt to Dorothy was a different matter. Her influence on him was different in kind, though just as great, and possibly even longer-lasting. She did not stir his social conscience, like Beaupuis, nor question him about poetic diction, like Coleridge. When he speaks of her, Wordsworth says she is like a 'brook'—yet another water-image—and that she accompanies him gently and quietly; her effect on him is gentle and unobtrusive. Yet the contribution which she made towards his poetry was very marked, though perhaps not so marked in the *Lyrical Ballads* as in the poems that followed them. It is now time to look at the particular direction in which she led her brother, and at the ways in which she preserved him as a poet.

5

Poems in Two Volumes

The first poems to show unmistakable signs of Dorothy's influence are the lyrics in the *Lyrical Ballads*, and of those most particularly the *Lucy* lyrics from the 1800 edition. In Wordsworth's next major publication, the *Poems in Two Volumes* of 1807, Dorothy's influence is far more striking and noticeable; the years they spent together have borne fruit. This collection contains nearly all his most famous and popular poems; when most people think of Wordsworth, they think of poems from these volumes, like *The Solitary Reaper*, *The Daffodils* and *My heart leaps up when I behold*. This is the really well-known Wordsworth, the Wordsworth that appears in every anthology and book of quotations. From the titles alone we can see at a glance a marked difference from the contents of the *Lyrical Ballads*. Here we have *To the Daisy*, *To the Celandine*, *To the Skylark*, *To the Cuckoo*, *To a Butterfly*, *The Sparrow's Nest*, and many more of the same kind. Here, in fact, is Wordsworth the nature-poet.

As a child and as a young man, Wordsworth had not taken much interest in the smaller details of nature, in celandines and buttercups and birds; he had preferred the wild and the grand, the craggy austere scenery of the Lakes and the Alps, and paid little attention to the small and homely. He was never to have a very good eye for detail, and actually made mistakes about the names of birds and plants; he never acquired Tennyson's or Browning's flair for minute accuracy. Dorothy, on the other hand, had the most remarkable powers of observation, and noticed the smallest, most insignificant changes in flowers and plants; she was in every sense a nature-lover, and she imparted her enthusiasms to her brother. In the nature poems of 1807 we see the result of their many walks and excursions together, and we see nature for the first time not as something grand and sinister and powerful, as it is in much of *The Prelude*, but as a source of pleasure, comfort and delight. Nature is no longer the stern admonisher of an errant child, but a garden full of enjoyment. Wordsworth himself is quite well aware of this change in his own outlook, and of the person to whom he owes it, for he makes constant reference to it. In *The Prelude*, for instance (Book 13, line 211) he describes himself as 'a rock with torrents roaring, with the clouds familiar', and says he admired only love and beauty that have 'terror in them'; but Dorothy, he says, came and softened down his sternness, and planted the crevices of the rock with flowers.

In another poem, *The Sparrow's Nest*, he makes the same point, though in a different way, and without the involved, elaborate imagery that he uses so frequently in *The Prelude*. This poem is in many ways typical of the 1807 volume; in it, he is referring to his early childhood, when the family was still united, before the death of both his parents caused his long separation from Dorothy (Emmeline is Dorothy; for some reason Wordsworth very rarely uses real names in his poetry):

> Behold, within the leafy shade,
> Those bright blue eggs together laid!
> On me the chance discovered sight
> Gleamed like a vision of delight.
> I started, seeming to espy
> The home, and sheltered bed,
> The Sparrow's dwelling, which, hard by
> My Father's house, in wet or dry
> My sister Emmeline and I
> Together visited.
> She looked at it and seemed to fear it;
> Dreading, though wishing, to be near it:

Such heart was in her, being then
A little Prattler among men.
The Blessing of my later years
Was with me when a boy:
She gave me eyes, she gave me ears;
And humble cares, and delicate fears;
A heart, the fountain of sweet tears;
And love, and thought, and joy.

It is easy to see why this kind of poem was so popular and appealed so strongly to the Victorian reader. Its subject, a sparrow's nest, is pretty and charming, and its language is in no way obscure. It paints a loving, tender picture of the little brother and sister, a picture far more in keeping with the Victorian ideal of childhood than the stubborn little boy in *Anecdote for Fathers* or the perverse little girl in *We Are Seven*. (By the time he wrote this poem, Wordsworth had babies of his own, which doubtless gives an added warmth to his early memories of his sister.) It shows nature as a source of 'delight' and 'joy', and above all it has no difficult philosophical message, and no objectionable revolutionary views on poverty, liberty and social injustice. It is not challenging; it is inoffensive. It is a long way from the deliberately provocative *Idiot Boy*.

These differences, as Wordsworth is saying in the poem, are the direct result of Dorothy's influence upon him. It was her extreme sensitivity that first taught him to notice the beauty of a sparrow's eggs; but for her he would probably not have discovered them. As a boy, he used to go bird-nesting and laying snares for wild creatures, instead of timidly admiring their beauty as Dorothy did. It was she who 'gave him eyes and gave him ears', and showed him the pleasure that could be found in such ordinary homely discoveries. She also taught him a new tenderness, which took the place of his boyish need for violent action and activity. In another, very similar poem called *To a Butterfly*, he describes how as children they would chase butterflies together; 'A very hunter did I rush upon the prey,' he says, while Dorothy, 'God love her, feared to brush the dust from off its wings'. She taught him to restrain his natural wildness and restlessness, and showed him the way to more passive and quiet satisfactions; if Beaupuis taught Wordsworth the rights of man, Dorothy taught him the rights of animals and flowers. The second lesson was less important than the first, possibly, but it was also far less troubling, and it inspired as much poetry.

THE DAFFODILS

As well as acting as her brother's housekeeper, cook, secretary, companion and constant admirer, Dorothy also found time to write a journal of her own, which reveals in intimate detail the closely-woven lives and thoughts of brother and sister. Amongst the biology notes and references to feather mattresses and boiled lamb chops, we find the raw material for many of William's poems: some of them, like *Beggars*, are really as much an account of Dorothy's experience as of his own, and many more refer to shared experiences. Perhaps the most famous example of all is the poem on the daffodils, 'I wandered lonely as a cloud'; Wordsworth and Dorothy saw these daffodils together, on one of their walks by the edge of the lake, and Dorothy gives a full and beautifully-written description of the scene in her journal. She wrote her description the very same day, whereas William's account was written slightly later—recollected, as he puts it, in tranquillity—but the mood which he captures in his poem is marked by all the qualities that sprang from his association with her; it is the kind of poem which he could not have written had he not learned to see through her eyes, although he makes no open reference to her in it, and in fact seems, oddly enough, to have forgotten that she was with him at the time.

The qualities that reveal Dorothy's influence most clearly are these. First and most obviously, the poem is about flowers, and, as we have seen, it was she who made him a flower-lover; it describes the kind of scene in which she took a particular delight, but which would not have impressed him nearly so strongly in the years before he came to know her. Secondly, as well as being about flowers, it uses the imagery of flowers, stars and clouds that Wordsworth first uses in the *Lucy* poems; the poet himself is as 'lonely as a cloud', the daffodils are 'continuous as the stars that shine and twinkle on the milky way'. Thirdly, it shows nature as a source not of power or terror, but of joy; it is essentially a happy scene, and the words *dancing, sprightly, glee, gay, jocund, bliss* and *pleasure* are all used, in an effort to describe the gaiety of both man and nature. And lastly, there is the way in which the experience of seeing the daffodils is stored up for future use, as a comfort for the years to come. The last verse describes this storage process in some detail; Wordsworth says that the sight of the daffodils has brought him more than a passing, momentary pleasure, and that he did not at first realize the value it would have for him:

> For oft, when on my couch I lie
> In vacant or in pensive mood,
> They flash upon that inward eye
> Which is the bliss of solitude;
> And then my heart with pleasure fills,
> And dances with the daffodils.   19-24

The daffodils, he says, will be a *lasting* source of pleasure to him; the memory of them will have the power to cheer and comfort him when he is idle or depressed. This is a notion which Wordsworth first expresses, mixed up with a lot of other ideas, in *Tintern Abbey*, and it is an idea that was to become stronger and stronger with him. Here it still has strength and vitality; the memory really can make his heart dance. But it is easy to see how this kind of attitude towards nature could degenerate, as it did eventually with Wordsworth, into an almost wholly passive attitude, so that in his middle and old age he is no longer drawing real strength from his memories, but is taking them out and turning them over as though they were old photographs, which can give some faint reflection of the thing that was, but never the thing itself. As a young man, Wordsworth's memories were far more to him than faded photographs; in *The Prelude*, when he speaks of drinking 'as from a fountain' or looking back to see the 'hiding places of his power' open to him again, he is speaking of a far more active, invigorating process. When he wrote *The Daffodils*, the process is still active, but only just so; he is already nearing the stage of life when nature can no longer fill him with overpowering joy and terror. It has become for him a pleasanter, milder thing altogether, a diversion rather than a part of himself. And in time it was to become even less than a diversion; it was to become little more than a refuge from and a consolation for the hardships of the world. We see in this poem, beautiful and carefully balanced as it is, hints of the later Wordsworth, of the man withdrawn from the world, who has lost interest in others, and who has retreated from the disturbing claims of genius and originality into a quiet country backwater, and into his own small devoted domestic circle.

FLOWERPIECES

It would of course be quite unjustifiable to blame Dorothy's influence for this eventual retreat; it has many other causes, which will be discussed later. Nor would it be fair to see all Wordsworth's flower poetry as poetry of a comforting and escapist kind; some of it is as bleak and harsh and honest as the early ballads. At this stage in his life, at the turning-point between youth and middle age, Wordsworth seems to have alternated between moods of happy, comfortable ease, and darker moods in which he senses the inevitable decline of his own health and genius; the two moods can be well illustrated by a comparison between two flower poems, both published in 1807: *To the Daisy* ('Bright flower, whose home is everywhere') and *The Small Celandine* ('There is a flower, the lesser celandine').

To the Daisy is not a very good poem; it shows the nature-lover Wordsworth at his worst. It does not attempt to describe any one particular scene, as the daffodil poem does; it is an apostrophe to daisies in general, and its tone is somewhat artificial. The poet praises the daisy for its homeliness, for its friendliness to all mankind, for being 'so meek and willing'; he says that man can learn humility from the daisy, he can learn to find a 'shelter from every wind', and ends up on a note of admiration for the flower which is content to grow unnoticed:

Meek, yielding to occasion's call,
And all things suffering from all,
Thy function apostolical
In peace fulfilling.   21-4

All in all, the poem is a very good example of what is meant by the 'pathetic fallacy'—that is, the attributing of human feelings and motives to non-human objects like flowers and rivers and animals. Wordsworth uses it a great deal, and it is one of his habits that those who dislike him dislike most strongly. In this case, they have reason to dislike it, for the whole poem is nothing but a pathetic fallacy; it has no contact with reality. Wordsworth can convince us that the daffodils did dance with joy, but he cannot convince us that a daisy is as saintly as to suffer all things for all—presumably all he means is that daisies get trodden on, though he does not say so. He assumes too much on the daisy's behalf, and he does not take the reader along with him; to use the religious word 'apostolical' about a mere flower is going a bit far, even the non-Christian might feel. It is fair enough to compare a saint or an apostle to a flower, but another matter to say a flower is like an apostle. Daisies are all very well in their own place, but they are not apostolical, whatever they are.

The Small Celandine is a very different and much better poem; it was obviously written in a very different mood. The first two verses describe, in a general way, the behaviour of celandines in bad spring weather, and how they will close up when the hailstones fall 'swarm on swarm'; these verses are unremarkably, plainly descriptive. The following verses, however, describe not the general habits of celandines, but a particular incident; the poet tells how he saw one day an old celandine, already on the verge of withering, which was too frail and old to shut its petals up in self-defence. Immediately one recognizes the real Wordsworth note, the extraordinary mixture of the accidental, personal moment—'lately, one rough day'—and the brooding mind of the man remembering the moment, working it out, feeling, wondering, concluding. Here are the last four verses:

> But lately, one rough day, this Flower I passed
> And recognised it, though an altered form,
> Now standing forth an offering to the blast,
> And buffeted at will by rain and storm.
>
> I stopped, and said with inly-muttered voice,
> 'It doth not love the shower, nor seek the cold:
> This neither is its courage nor its choice,
> But its necessity in being old.
>
> 'The sunshine may not cheer it, nor the dew;
> It cannot help itself in its decay;
> Stiff in its members, withered, changed of hue.'
> And in my spleen, I smiled that it was grey.
>
> To be a Prodigal's Favourite—then, worse truth,
> A miser's Pensioner—behold our lot!
> O Man, that from thy fair and shining youth,
> Age might but take the things Youth needed not!   9-24

Unlike the daisy piece, this is real, first-hand poetry. This 'inly-muttered voice' is the voice of Wordsworth's poetic middle-age, the voice of a man often worried, often depressed, often regretful, and with little interest in cheering himself up. The meaning of the poem is simple enough; it is a cold, bleak look at old age. Noticeably, Wordsworth does not attribute all kinds of unlikely human emotions to the celandine; the emotions are all his own. There is no strained pathetic fallacy, but an entirely natural, unforced comparison between man's life and the flower's. The flower, he says, is not choosing to suffer, it is not showing any human bravery in failing to protect itself; being old, it cannot help but suffer. '*It cannot help itself in its decay*'. Note that this last sentence, Wordsworth's own, needs no translation from poetry into prose; the words, and the word-order are natural and inevitable. Yet they are not prosaic; the whole poem has the ring of classic simplicity and finality; it has dignity without pomposity. The lines:

> This neither is its courage nor its choice
> But its necessity in being old

are a classic summary of the helpless dignity of old age, a state which touches Wordsworth with a peculiarly deep feeling.

The imagery of the poem has the same simple inevitability as the language. The parallel between man's life and the flower's— by no means a new one—is worked out with a fresh but unstrained aptness. All the words which Wordsworth uses to describe the flower's state apply equally well to man's, but it is not until the third line of the third verse quoted that he strikes a specifically human note; when he says 'Stiff in its members, withered, changed of hue', the reader can no longer avoid the picture of a stiff, grey-haired, wrinkled old man, although all the words apply equally well to the sapless, stiff, faded flower. The parallel is not pushed upon the reader; it arises naturally in his own mind, in time to prepare him for the final verse.

The last verse draws the moral. It is a plain moral conclusion, the kind of (trite) conclusion so dear to inferior poets, but it is made here with force and meaning, not with an air of pious duty. It tells us what is, not what ought to be. And Wordsworth really means it; his conclusion is as much a heart-felt cry as a neatly worked out ending. It is not the thought itself which is new, for the thought is trite enough—when we are young, we have too much, too many riches to appreciate or use them properly, and when we are old we have too little, and are forced to live on charity, physically if not financially. This has been said many times before, but the point is that Wordsworth says it here with conviction, in a new way, as though it had newly occurred to him that he too would grow old and helpless and dependent; the phrase 'fair and shining youth', with its direct reference back to the golden petals of the flower, remind us of the occasion which brought this new awareness into his mind. The moral arises

entirely naturally out of the incident; it is not tagged on point-
lessly. Nor is the incident told merely for the sake of a good
moral; it is real and vivid in itself, and we cannot doubt that this
poem was written, in Wordsworth's phrase, with 'the eye on the
object'. It is about a dying flower on a real raw spring day, not
about flowers in general. It is both an encounter with a real
flower, and the encounter of a middle-aged man with the threat
of old-age; it is the unstrained and natural combination of symbol
and meaning that make it such a good and effective poem.

POETRY OF RESIGNATION

The Small Celandine is a good introduction to Wordsworth's
last great poetic phase, and to his last great poetic inspiration.
We have seen that, as a young man, his poetry rose from two
main sources: from his faith and hopes for the future of man and
society, and from his keen sense of communion with nature. As
he grew older, these two springs of energy dried up in him, and
he was to write a great mass of verse between the ages of forty
and eighty which is almost totally lacking in energy, originality
and inspiration. Most people have thought that he simply did not
notice his failure of inspiration, and that he went on writing with
a blind and happy conviction that he was still turning out great
works. There are, however, clear signs that in the second half of
his life he suffered from deep depression and disillusion, which
he did his best to regulate and conceal, with considerable
success. There is a group of poems, written while he was still at
the height of his powers, which seem to forecast this approaching
decline, and which are full of evidence that he knew what was
happening to himself as a poet; they are all remarkably similar
in feeling if not in actual meaning. They are poems written not
with joy, nor about joy, but about the loss of joy. They are
poems about the problem of living without joy.

The most important poems in this group are *Resolution and
Independence*, often known as *The Leech Gatherer* (written 1802,
published 1807), *Ode to Duty* (written 1804, published 1807),
Ode on the Intimations of Immortality from Recollections of Early

117

Childhood (written over a few years, probably 1802–4, and published 1807), and *Elegiac Stanzas suggested by a picture of Peele Castle in a Storm* (written 1805, published 1807). These poems, different as they are, all share a certain stiff determination to make the best of things, to carry on without complaining, and they all lament the loss of the easy spontaneous joys and passions of early youth.

Resolution and Independence, the first written of the group, seems to be almost like a premonition of what was to come. It was written at an apparently prosperous and joyful time of his life, while he was at the height of his poetic powers—technically and imaginatively, it is one of his finest works—and yet it tells of threats and dangers and endurance. It starts off optimistically enough: it is the morning after a heavy storm, and Wordsworth is off on one of his solitary walks. Both he and the world around him are full of joy and life; the grass is 'bright with rain drops', the hare is 'running races in her mirth', the lark is singing, and the poet is as light-hearted and happy as a boy. As he walks, he says he forgets all his troubles:

> My old remembrances went from me wholly;
> And all the ways of men, so vain and melancholy.
>
> 19–20

But as he continues his walk, he is quite suddenly and for no apparent reason plunged into the deepest gloom; his happy mood turns quite involuntarily to 'dim sadness' and 'blind thoughts'. In the depths of this acute and irrational fit of depression, he starts to imagine all the dangers that might possibly threaten his present happiness, and which did overwhelm the lives of other poets; he thinks of Chatterton, 'the marvellous boy', who committed suicide, and of Burns, who died while still young in poverty and sickness. As he contemplates these disasters, he imagines them happening to himself; he says that although he himself is now as carefree as the lark and the hare:

> there may come another day to me—
> Solitude, pain of heart, distress and misery—

—and he goes on to compare his own lot with the lot of other poets, saying:

> We poets in our youth begin in gladness;
> But thereof come in the end despondency and madness.

48–9

He is not speaking here of purely physical hardships, but of mental failures; he seems to imply that it is the very intensity of joy itself, the violent gladness of the young poet, which wears him out and plunges him later into sorrow and misery. He fears that the moods of exaltation described in *The Prelude* may be paid for in the end. (Wordsworth aged early, his friends said, and they said it was because his spirit and energy burned him out.) He seems in this part of the poem to be foreseeing the loss of his own powers, and to be dreading the fate of unseeing mediocrity in store for him.

But then, as he wanders along in this mood of vague but deep forebodings, he comes upon the leech gatherer. This leech gatherer is the strangest and most impressive of all Wordsworth's many portraits of old age, and he appears mysteriously, as though by divine intervention. He is a warning, a portent, an admonition; the poet feels at once that he has some message for him, and that his appearance there in that lonely place is not without meaning. When he first sees him, he is standing alone and motionless by a pool, and Wordsworth describes him in this famous and striking image:

> As a huge stone is sometimes seen to lie
> Couched on the bald top of an eminence;
> Wonder to all who do the same espy,
> By what means it could thither come, and whence;
> So that it seems a thing endued with sense:
> Like a sea-beast crawled forth, that on a shelf
> Of rock or sand reposeth, there to sun itself;
>
> Such seemed this Man, not all alive nor dead,
> Nor all asleep—in his extreme old age:

His body was bent double, feet and head
Coming together in life's pilgrimage;
As if some dire constraint of pain, or rage
Of sickness felt by him in times long past,
A more than human weight upon his frame had cast.

57–70

These images, of the 'huge stone', and of the 'sea-beast crawled forth', make the old man at once a part of the landscape, a natural, almost inanimate object, and yet at the same time an object of wonder and mystery, whose very presence is a cause for wonder. Wordsworth watches this strange impressive figure, standing there motionless propped on his staff staring into the pool, and then, in typically Wordsworthian fashion, he proceeds to question him, just as he questioned the disbanded soldier, and the little girl in *We Are Seven*. He asks what the man is doing in such a lonely place, and what occupation he is pursuing. The leech gatherer replies in a feeble voice, but with dignity; his words are 'solemn', 'stately', 'measured', 'lofty'. He says that, being old and poor, he does what he can to earn his living by wandering the moors from pond to pond collecting leeches to sell. As he replies, the poet's attention wanders, and he drifts off once more into his own private depression; he still dimly hears the leech gatherer's voice in the back of his mind, 'like a stream scarce heard', while he ponders on his own fears, on:

cold, pain and labour, and all fleshly ills
And mighty poets in their misery dead.

115–16

The leech gatherer is not forgotten; he is present 'like one whom I had met with in a dream', and his own fears and the leech gatherer's tale of uncomplaining hardship blend into an extraordinary visionary sense of dim trouble and dim comfort. Wordsworth, when he pulls himself out of his reverie, asks the old man to go over his story again, just as he asked the little girl and the little boy in *Anecdote for Fathers* to repeat their answers again and again. The old man patiently repeats himself, and Wordsworth says that when he ended:

> I could have laughed myself to scorn to find
> In that decrepit Man so firm a mind.
> 'God', said I, 'be my help and stay secure;
> I'll think of the Leech-gatherer on the lonely moor.'

137–40

And on this note the poem too ends. It is an extraordinary and powerful work, with the same strange distance between meaning and argument that appears in passages of *The Prelude*. On one level, Wordsworth seems to be saying something like this: 'One day, while out for a walk, I fell into a mood of unaccountable depression and anxiety. Then I met an old leech gatherer, who was so old and so poor and so much worse off than me that I felt guilty about feeling sorry for myself, and in future every time I start to feel sorry for myself I will think of that poor old man.' And in one way, this is precisely what Wordsworth does mean, but a crude summary like this misses out everything that makes the poem important. Once again, it is not the thought that counts, for the thought is trite enough; it is the circumstances. It is the figure of the old man himself which makes the poem so remarkable. He is at once real and symbolic, a real old man and a portent of something else. It is his dignity more than his poverty that impresses Wordsworth; he is very much the poet's superior in the virtues of resolution and independence mentioned in the poem's title, and the poet feels awe and admiration for him, not pity. He is not saying, 'Thank God I am not as badly off as he is', but rather hoping that he may bear whatever comes to him with like honour. The old man, like the black cliffs that towered above the boy Wordsworth in the stolen boat, or like the 'low breathings' that warned him off when he stole birds from other boys' snares, is a force of nature; he impresses Wordsworth not by what he *says* but by what he *is*.

This poem is a good example of what people mean when they speak of Wordsworth's 'profound simplicity'. At first sight, there is nothing complicated about it at all. The moral of 'count your blessings' appears to be straightforward enough. The story and its setting are simple; the moor, the pond, the racing hare, the weather and the old man himself are all described in very plain language. The one real event of the poem, Wordsworth's encounter with the old man, is outwardly at least the most ordinary sort of occurrence. In fact, to some people the whole poem seems ludicrously simple, and trivial to the point of insignificance; Wordsworth had to defend it himself to his close friend and admirer, his wife's sister Sarah, who found the leech gatherer's ramblings 'tedious'. He wrote to her with indignation:

> It is in the character of the old man to tell his story in a manner which an *impatient* reader must necessarily find tedious. But Good God, Such a figure, in such a place, a pious, self-respecting, miserably infirm Old Man telling such a tale.

That phrase—'such a figure, in such a place'—is the clue to the whole poem's power; it is the time and the place, the circumstances, the reality of the situation that make the difference between a profound truth and a boring commonplace. What the leech gatherer says may be simple and tedious enough, but its meaning in the context of the whole poem is new and weighty.

The *Ode to Duty* is a much less impressive poem. It is abstract in subject and language, full of phrases addressed to a personified Duty, such as 'dread power' and 'stern lawgiver', which are rhetorical in a way that the *Leech Gatherer* never is, and which appeal hardly at all to the imagination. But it does have a similarity of mood. In it, Wordsworth regrets the time when he did the right thing easily and instinctively:

> When love is an unerring light
> And joy its own security.

19–20

Those days are over, and instead of trusting to love and joy, the poet has to trust to his sense of duty. He longs for 'a repose

122

that ever is the same', a repose that is a faint reminder of the leech gatherer's stoic dignity. He tries to resign himself to accepting his Duty with joy, but does not seem entirely happy about the prospect; the mood of the poem is altogether somewhat austere and depressing. However, although a little strained both in language and sentiment, its message is clear enough.

The *Ode on the Intimations* is another matter altogether. It is neither easy nor clear. It has neither the simple story basis of the *Leech Gatherer*, nor the clearly developed argument of the *Ode to Duty*. It is wholly irregular in stanza form and rhyme scheme, and its language jumps without warning from the simple to the conventionally poetic to the philosophical, and back again. Its very title is enough to warn the reader that it is hardly the most straightforward of poems, and its meanings have been the source of endless discussion. Despite these difficulties, however, it has always been a popular piece for teaching in schools, partly because of its evident importance, and partly perhaps because it appears to deal with the subject of childhood, a subject which is supposed to appeal to the young. In fact, it is not really about childhood at all; it is about the death of childhood and the loss of joy, and it is extremely difficult for young people to sympathize with it at all. It is essentially a middle-aged poem, and for Wordsworth it is something of a swan song. He does his best to close it on a note of optimism and hope, but nevertheless what comes across most powerfully from the poem is a feeling of anguished regret for what is lost. However nobly he resolves to bear his loss, resolution itself can never make up for what is gone, and he knows it.

The poem opens with a perfectly straightforward statement. There was a time, Wordsworth says, when meadow, grove and stream seemed to be 'apparelled in celestial light', and that time is now over. He makes no qualifications, just the blank statement. Apart from the words 'apparelled', 'celestial' and 'yore', every word in the first stanza is in everyday use, and even those three words are not particularly rare. The last line of the stanza is as simply expressed as anything Wordsworth ever wrote:

'The things which I have seen I now can see no more', he says; every word is monosyllabic, every word is as ordinary as can be. The poet's meaning, so far, cannot be mistaken, and in this opening stanza he expresses the theme of the whole *Ode*—the theme of lost vision.

In the second stanza, he develops the point. Nature itself, he says, is still as beautiful as it ever was: the rainbow, the rose, the sun, moon and stars are still there, and still beautiful. It is he that has changed, not they; for him, the glory has gone. Then, in the third stanza, this feeling of simple loss starts to change into something else; it starts to change into a feeling of guilt. He feels that even if he cannot see the glory he once saw, he *ought* to be able to. He is ashamed to be the only sad creature in the gay spring-time world, and he sees his sadness as a blot on the landscape, so he resolves to be happy. 'No more shall grief of mine the season wrong,' he says, determining to share the beauty of spring and not to spoil it by withdrawing into his own melancholy. But there is more determination than spontaneous gaiety, even in his language; words like 'festival', 'coronal' and 'jubilee' are not words that he would have chosen to describe the beauty of nature in his earlier poems. He is willing himself to be happy, and the note is forced; at the end of the fourth stanza he admits as much, forgetting about the joyful shepherd boys and his duty not to complain, and saying, with an almost blank, simple regret:

> But there's a Tree, of many, one,
> A single Field which I have looked upon,
> Both of them speak of something that is gone.   51–3

He does not even bother to say it was an exceptionally beautiful tree, or a particularly interesting field; it is just a tree, just a field. The 'visionary gleam' which used to light the whole face of the earth for him when as a boy he was out skating, or when he visited Tintern Abbey as a young man, has now faded for ever. He may try to see it, even make pretence that he can see it, but it is gone.

This loss of the brilliant, highly-coloured vision of childhood is also described by the twentieth-century Welsh poet, Dylan Thomas, in one of his best poems, *Fern Hill*; Thomas too had happy memories of childhood in the country and he writes of the magic brightness of his early years when he was 'young and easy under the apple boughs', and 'prince of the apple towns'. But he too is aware, though perhaps less painfully than Wordsworth, that this brightness must fade; the sun, he says, is 'young once only', and the children follow the sun 'out of grace'. From earliest infancy, even though we are quite unaware of it, we are in the grip of Time; Thomas expresses this sense of limited ecstasy very beautifully in the last two lines of his poem, where he says that:

> Time held me green and dying
> Though I sang in my chains like the sea.

FERN HILL

The whole poem makes a very interesting comparison with the *Immortality Ode*, for the two poets are trying to describe similar emotions, though in very different idioms.

It is not until the fifth stanza of the *Ode* that Wordsworth embarks upon philosophy; the first four stanzas are lyrical and emotional, offering no reasons or explanations. The middle section of the *Ode*, beginning with 'Our birth is but a sleep and a forgetting', gives Wordsworth's philosophy of childhood; here, more than anywhere else in his works, he tries to reduce his scattered impressions and convictions into an orderly system. His philosophy has been compared to Plato's, but it is in fact less of an abstract system than a description of his own personal experience of life and the process of ageing. Briefly, his theory seems to be something like this: the new born soul does not come from nowhere, out of nothingness, but from some other ill-defined country—'from afar', 'from an imperial palace'. (This is a fairly common conviction, held by mystics of various religions.) The little child still has clear memories and visions of this other, heavenly place, but as he grows older they begin to fade. Earth does her best to make him forget this other place, and its glories, and the child himself tries (unwisely) to hurry on this process of forgetfulness, longing to be grown up, playing at being a grown-up, imitating adults in his games. Eventually he does grow up and forget, though he goes through a period when he still has rare glimpses of memory and vision, though unable to keep in constant contact with his sense of glory. When he is fully mature, even these glimpses are lost and 'fade into the light of common day'. On one level, this is a plain description of Wordsworth's own progress from childhood through youth to a somewhat bleak and disillusioned middle age; it is the same story that *The Prelude* tells. It is only Wordsworth's attempts to make his own experiences into a general philosophy, applicable to all men, and true of the whole human condition, that make the *Ode* confusing; Wordsworth was no philosopher, though he felt he ought to be one. His mind never dealt as easily in abstract ideas as it did with some massive single physical symbol like the leech gatherer.

The real weakness of his philosophizing comes out most strongly in a passage like the beginning of the eighth stanza, which addresses the child as :

> Thou, whose exterior semblance doth belie
>   Thy Soul's immensity;
> Thou best philosopher, who yet dost keep
> Thy heritage, thou Eye among the blind,
> That, deaf and silent, reads't the eternal deep . . .
> Mighty prophet! Seer blest . . .
>
> 109–15

This is both obscure and a little pretentious; in calling children 'best philosophers' and 'seers blest', he is overloading his subject in much the same way as when he calls daisies apostolical. Children have wisdom of a kind, but not of this kind. And to whom or what do the words 'deaf and silent' refer?

In the last section of the poem, having explained his theory of childhood, Wordsworth is left with the task of telling us how to carry on when we are no longer children. If, as he says, all life is a continual decline and the process of ageing is a process of inevitable decay, from birth onwards, what are we supposed to do about it? We cannot remain children forever, like Peter Pan, nor can we just sit down and resign ourselves to growing older and sadder. It is a very real problem, and Wordsworth warns the child of its gravity when he says:

> Full soon thy Soul shall have her earthly freight,
> And custom lie upon thee with a weight,
> Heavy as frost, and deep almost as life.

127–9

There is no mistaking the note of deep depression in these lines; custom clearly is oppressing Wordsworth in reality, as it did in imagination in *The Leech Gatherer*. His natural joy is freezing up; he is losing his moments of vision, and with them his poetic genius, and he knows it.

However, he does not end on this note of despondency. He goes on to express gratitude for the little that is left, and for the glory of what has been, and says he will:

> grieve not, rather find
> Strength in what remains behind;
> In the primal sympathy
> Which having been must ever be;
> In the soothing thoughts that spring
> Out of human suffering;
> In the faith that looks through death,
> In years that bring the philosophic mind.

180–7

This is comfort, but it is cold comfort. It is impossible to read the last verses of the *Ode* as an expression of real light-heartedness; he says that the radiance that was once so bright is now *forever* taken from his sight, and when he says—

> O joy! that in our embers
> Is *something* that doth live,

130–7

—he is not pretending to prefer the embers to the full blaze he used to know; he is merely expressing his humble thanks that there is a little trace of heat left amongst the ashes. He was to sit by those embers for the next forty years, raking them over and over, but the best that he was to find was little more than a few sparks in comparison with what had been. It was a sad future, and a depressing one for a great poet, but, being what he was, he endured it with dignity and integrity, and without great bursts of bitterness or self-pity. He was the least self-pitying, the least self-romanticizing of men, and he kept on trying, even after most of the pleasure of effort had gone.

This *Immortality Ode* shows the best and the weakest of Wordsworth. It has in parts the deep, powerful, simply-expressed emotion of his greatest works, and yet it also shows signs of the weaknesses that were to become more and more common in his poems—abstractions, artificialities of language, apostrophes, personifications, inflated thoughts and fancies, forced piety and gaiety, and all the trappings of bad eighteenth-century verse that he had begun his career by rejecting. It is a remarkable mixture, and a more personal poem than is some-times realized.

The last of this group of poems about resignation is different from the others in that it was written not about a vague sense of growing age and loss, but about a specific tragedy. It is called, to give it its full title, *Elegiac Stanzas suggested by a Picture of Peele Castle in a Storm, painted by Sir George Beaumont*, and it was written in 1805, as an elegy for Wordsworth's brother John who had died that year when his ship was lost at sea. The tragedy of John's death was a dreadful blow to William and Dorothy; he was their favourite brother, far closer to them than the other two, Christopher and Richard, and they never got over the shock of his tragic, unexpected fate. With his death, a chapter in their lives was closed; the carefree optimism of youth was felt to be gone for ever.

The connection between John's death and a painting of a castle in a storm is not at first obvious. Wordsworth opens the poem by saying that once, years ago, he spent four summer weeks by this very castle, and that if he had been a painter and had painted it then, he would not have chosen a stormy background, but would have painted it:

> Beside a sea that could not cease to smile;
> On tranquil land, beneath a sky of bliss.

19–20

But, with John's death, the days when he could see it in such a way are over; he will never again paint such a picture of joy and peace:

> A power is gone, which nothing can restore;
> A deep distress hath humanised my Soul.
>
> Not for a moment could I now behold
> A smiling sea, and be what I have been:
> The feeling of my loss will ne'er be old.

35–9

He goes on to say that Beaumont's picture of the castle in the storm now seems truer to him than the smiling scene which he himself saw as a young man, and he praises the artist's courage in showing things as they are. The storm—'the lightning, the fierce wind, the trampling waves'—all remind him painfully of the dreadful night when his brother lost his life, but he says he will not try to escape the memory of his loss; he will face it like a man, and try to gain from it in human sympathy and understanding. The last verse, strikingly plain in language, is full of a noble resignation:

> But welcome, fortitude, and patient cheer,
> And frequent sights of what is to be borne!
> Such sights, or worse, as are before me here—
> Not without hope we suffer and we mourn.

57–60

Once more, we hear the note of *determination*; Wordsworth is a man of will power, and he will face the grimness of tragedy without dishonesty. Life is bad, but it must be borne, and if we are to bear it then we must look it in the face. The castle and the storm are physical reminders of death, just as the leech gatherer is a reminder of pain, poverty and age. Death is a fact, and it has dispelled the bright and dazzling weather of youth, 'the light that never was on sea or land'; there is no point in trying to evade reality. It is much better to strengthen ourselves by contemplating it with fortitude.

There is also, in the last line of this poem, something like a note of Christian hope. From this time on, Wordsworth, who had never been an orthodox Christian, was to become a churchgoer. There can be no doubt that it was partly at least the shock of John's death that turned him towards the comfort of Christianity, as the fact of death turns so many, and this is one of the first hints of his final total conversion and commitment.

6

Poetic Decline

Everyone agrees about the inferiority of Wordsworth's later work, though there is little agreement about the date at which inferiority set in. Several of his later works have been much admired: the River Duddon *Sonnets*, for example, a series published in 1820, were very popular during his lifetime, and the *White Doe of Rylstone*, a historical romance, has its enthusiasts even today. There are one or two miscellaneous sonnets, such as *Surprised by joy, impatient as the wind*, which are of as fine a quality as anything he ever wrote. *The Excursion*, his longest, most ambitious and most philosophical poem, which was published in 1814, has some very good passages, but the poem as a whole is little read today, and its finest part, the first book, does not belong to Wordsworth's later period at all, but was written as a separate poem, *The Ruined Cottage*, well before he was thirty. It was *The Excursion*, however, which established his reputation as an important poet to his contemporaries; ironically, as is so often the case, he began to receive widespread recognition just as his powers began to decline.

The poetry which he wrote during and after his decline differs from his earlier work in its extremely commonplace and timid sentiments, and its extreme artificiality of language. The two seem to go together. It is a wonder that such a passionate believer in social equality could ever have brought himself to write sonnets in praise of landed gentry, the death penalty and the Church of England, but he did. It is a wonder that the author of the *Lyrical Ballads*, with his bold views on poetic diction, could ever have produced a line like:

—(a line at least as bad as Cowper's prize example of eighteenth-century poetic diction, which refers to hens as 'the feathered tribe domestic')—but he did. How did this change take place? How did the outspoken radical turn into the timid Tory? How did the mighty original of *The Prelude* and the *Lyrical Ballads* manage to produce so much feeble verse about ladies' needle cases and lovely sunsets?

The change was, of course, partly due to the natural process of time. A loss of faith in social progress and human equality is extremely common in middle age, and to one who had seen, as Wordsworth had seen, the violent horrors of the French Revolution, and the worse terrors of Napoleon's conquests, it was natural enough. And, added to this change in political faith and hope, there was the change in his own personal situation. He was no longer a young man without responsibilities, but a middle-aged man with a family to keep. He married in 1802, at the late age of thirty-two, and by the time he was forty he had had five children. He was not a rich man; his marriage, though happy, was not a passionate one, and it was a steadying rather than a stirring influence.

As he grew older, too, his circle of friends began to change. In his poetic prime, his greatest friend was Coleridge, who was a stimulating, difficult, provoking companion, but never a dull one. Coleridge, however, led a tormented and unhappy life; he suffered from continual ill-health and from the opium he took to cure his ill-health; he could not live with his own wife, he quarrelled with all his friends, including the Wordsworths, and he lost his poetic gifts in a far more dramatic way than Wordsworth did. The spectacle of his wretched wanderings, his profound unhappiness and dreadful nightmares, may well have persuaded Wordsworth that it would be better to stay quietly at home and look after his family and aim at peace and harmony rather than at such dangerous freedom. Considering the calm domestic picture we have of Wordsworth's family circle and friends, it is surprising how much oddity, illness and insanity it had on its fringes. Dorothy herself fell ill in 1829 and never recovered, either mentally or physically, though she outlived her brother. One friend, Charles Lloyd, went insane and was put in an institution; another, Charles Lamb, devoted his life to looking after his sister Mary, who in a fit of insanity had murdered their mother in his presence. De Quincey, who was to become a close friend and neighbour, took opium like Coleridge, and was thoroughly neurotic even without its help. With such examples before his eyes, one can well believe that Wordsworth valued peace and serenity and family duties at the expense of a more turbulent, unsettled way of life, which might have made him a better poet, though not necessarily a better man.

Typical of the new circle of friends and influences amongst which he began to move at this period in his life is Sir George Beaumont, who painted the picture of Peele Castle which he refers to in the poem on the death of his brother. Sir George was quite unlike the friends of his early youth. He was fifteen years older than Wordsworth, and from an ancient landed family; he was interested in painting and literature, and spent some of his money in patronizing artists whom he admired. By all accounts he and his wife were a pleasant, intelligent, well-informed couple. Coleridge first drew Wordsworth's work to their attention, and they made their first offer of help (a plot of land in the Lake District) in 1803; Wordsworth accepted it, though with some delay and embarrassment. But as time went on their friendship prospered, and within three or four years Wordsworth and his family were staying for months at a time at Sir George's country house, Coleorton; Wordsworth advised him on his landscape garden, wrote him long letters and some rather inferior verse, and in short accepted his life-long patronage. In such a position, there was clearly a need not to offend Sir George's conservative political views, although there was no obligation to repeat them; Wordsworth could not bite the hand that fed him. Also, he doubtless did not want to bite this particular hand, for Sir George represented all that was most agreeable in English upper-class society, and Wordsworth genuinely liked and admired him. In becoming Sir George's friend, he certainly did not sell his soul for money, as his more radical friends and enemies insinuated. However, this friendship was another step towards his transformation into the anti-Reform Bill, anti-Roman Catholic, anti-French, anti-Whig, thoroughly pro-Establishment figure of his old age. Sir George was an excellent friend for a family man, but perhaps not such a good friend for an independent poet.

From this point in his life onwards, Wordsworth became more and more deeply embedded in English social life, and made fewer protests against the injustices that had seemed so clear to him as a young man. He accepted a Government post in 1813, as Distributor of Stamps for Westmorland, which involved little work and a good income; thirty years later he was to accept, though under protest, that final distinction of the socially accepted poet, the Poet Laureateship. He lived surrounded by a close and devoted family circle, children, grandchildren, sisters-in-law, friends and admirers. In the eyes of the world he was a success, and he did what was expected of him. And yet, when we read of his later life, we cannot feel that we are reading about a happy man; the picture we get is of a brooding, solitary, dis-illusioned and often profoundly miserable man. As late as 1817, when he was forty-seven, he could still write a poem quite passionate in its regret for lost power: this poem, *Composed on an Evening of Extraordinary Splendour and Beauty*, is well worth looking at for proof that Wordsworth was not blissfully unaware of his fading talent. Although the language of most of it is horribly poetic in a bad sense—full of lines like 'Thine is the tranquil hour, purpureal Eve'—the passion shines through the artificiality of the words. He prays to God to—

> let Thy grace remind me of the light
> Full early lost, and fruitlessly deplored. 73–4

These are not the words of a complacent man, but of a poet condemned to a life of resignation and hard work. He bore his state with more dignity than Coleridge, and with less annoyance to his friends and relatives, but he was not happy. If he had died young, as Keats, Shelley and Byron did, we would have a very different picture of him today; but he survived, and we have to try to understand the older man without forgetting our admiration for the younger one.

It would not be fair to leave this account of Wordsworth's decline as a poet without some acknowledgement of his later style. *Laodamia*, for instance, written in 1814, has been generally thought to be a fine and successful poem, and it is successful, though in quite a different manner from his earlier work. It is on a subject taken from the Greek classics; we remember that one of the things Wordsworth objected to most strongly in eighteenth-century poetry was all the meaningless classical decoration of graces, goddesses, nymphs and so forth. His own use of shepherds and idiot boys had been a protest against this very fashion, yet here we find him using it himself. He uses it, however, to some purpose; the story of *Laodamia*, though cool, restrained, and removed from everyday life, is in its own way moving. Laodamia is the wife of the first Greek warrior to die at Troy; the gods allow him to return to earth for a brief space to console her. He preaches patience and resignation, a favourite lesson of the ageing Wordsworth, who had by this time lost a brother and two of his own children; he tells her that:

> the Gods approve
> The depth, and not the tumult, of the soul.   74–5

The whole mood of the poem is one of dignified, heroic restraint; it is cool and disembodied, with none of the prosaic details that make the restraint of *Michael* or *The Brothers* or *The Leech Gatherer* so convincing. Nevertheless, it is a good poem, and better than many of the Greek tales of Tennyson and Matthew Arnold, who, like Wordsworth, returned to the classics, in refuge from the gross and ugly problems of their own day.

Hazlitt, a contemporary of Wordsworth and a famous critic, sums up the difference between Wordsworth's early and later style extremely well. He praises the early works with real understanding, describes Wordsworth's power of 'dealing with the simplest feelings of the heart' in subjects that may appear trifling or ridiculous, and goes on to say:

> His later philosophic productions have a somewhat different character. They are a departure from, a dereliction of, his first principles. They are classical and courtly. They are polished in style, without being gaudy; dignified in subject, without affectation. They seem to have been composed not in a cottage at Grasmere, but among the half-inspired groves and stately recollections of Coleorton.
>
> THE SPIRIT OF THE AGE, Chapter on Wordsworth

Hazlitt is surely right when he makes this link between the change in Wordsworth's way of life and the change in his poetry. The two things were inseparable.

7

Critics and Biographers

Wordsworth has long been recognized as a great and important poet. Even during his lifetime, he was the centre of a circle of devoted Wordsworthians, in whose eyes he could do no wrong. Such respectful admiration was probably not very good for him, and doubtless encouraged him in the less agreeable habits of his old age, such as talking too seriously about himself, and too harshly about his fellow-poets. However, not all his critics were admirers; his early work was violently attacked, and even the well-received *Excursion* inspired a celebrated review (by Jeffrey, in the *Edinburgh Review*) beginning: 'This will never do'. But perhaps it is one of his peculiar distinctions to have been one of the most parodied of all great poets. Writers do not seem to be able to resist taking him off, and it is very easy to make him look silly; this is partly because he is not a polished poet, except in later works like *Laodamia*. His style at its greatest rests on a combination of the profound and the everyday, and a certain clumsiness is an essential part of it. It is very difficult to parody a sophisticated poet like Pope, who has an inbuilt irony which warns off lesser poets, but Wordsworth, with his deliberate disregard of elegance, lays himself open to attack.

Some of the attacks are very amusing. The earliest known parody is called the *Simpliciad*, and it was published anonymously in 1808, shortly after the *Poems in Two Volumes*. It is a witty, sophisticated piece in Pope-like heroic couplets, addressed to Wordsworth, Southey and Coleridge, who, because they all happened to live in the Lake District, were lumped together as 'The Lake School of Poets', although they had little in common; Wordsworth and Southey at this point did not even like each other. They acquired the label quite accidentally, much as a quite dissimilar group of writers became labelled 'Angry Young Men' in the 1950s. The unknown parodist addresses his poem to these three poets, saying: 'I have employed no unfair exaggeration: the school is incapable of caricature . . .' His objections to Wordsworth are clear enough: he finds him uncivilized, childish, unworldly. He mocks:

> Poets, who fix their visionary sight
> On sparrows' eggs in prospect of delight,
> With fervent welcome greet the glow-worm's flame,
> Put it to bed, and bless it by its name,
> Hunt waterfalls, and gallop down the hills,
> And dance with dancing laughing daffodils.
> Or measure muddy ponds from side to side
> And find them three feet long and two feet wide . . .
> Whine over tattered cloaks and ragged breeches,
> And moralize with gatherers of leeches. . . .

—and goes on to exclaim:

> See, with impassioned flowers each bank is teeming;
> See, with blue sparrow's eggs each hedge is gleaming;
> Ecstatic birds, whose thought no bard can measure,
> Blossoms that breathe, and twigs that pant with pleasure.

This is a fair, intelligent and witty attack, from someone with different but nevertheless high standards of literary taste: the attack on the pathetic fallacy, on 'twigs that pant with pleasure', is particularly well-aimed. This critic is not the kind of man to be understanding about apostolic daisies.

BYRON AND SHELLEY

Wordsworth was also ridiculed from a similarly sophisticated viewpoint by his contemporaries, Byron and Shelley. These two, both romantic, aristocratic, handsome men of the world, were quite well aware of Wordsworth's greatness, but they both thought him to be something of a country bumpkin, in his

138

poems and in his way of life. Byron attacks him in his long satiric poem, *English Bards and Scotch Reviewers* (in which, it is fair to say, he attacks almost every other living poet); this poem, like the *Simpliciad*, is in heroic couplets, and it too lumps Wordsworth with Southey—it even has the nerve to call Wordsworth Southey's 'disciple'. Here is what Byron says:

> Next comes the dull disciple of the school,
> That mild apostate from poetic rule,
> The simple Wordsworth, framer of a lay
> As soft as evening in his favourite May. . . .
> Who both by precept and example shows
> That prose is verse and verse is merely prose. . . .
> Thus, when he tells the tale of Betty Foy,
> The idiot mother of an idiot boy,
> A moon-struck, silly boy, who lost his way
> And, like his bard, confounded night with day;
> So close on each pathetic part he dwells
> And each adventure so sublimely tells
> That all who view 'the idiot in his glory'
> Conceive the bard the hero of the story.

235–54

Byron here portrays Wordsworth as a harmless simpleton; he chooses *The Idiot Boy* for special attack because it offends his aristocratic notion of good taste, and also because it provides such an easy target. The joke about Wordsworth being his own idiot hero is a very easy, feeble joke, like a pun on someone's name, and not nearly as revealing or shrewd an observation as the *Simpliciad*'s 'twigs that pant with pleasure'.

Shelley's parody of Wordsworth is an interesting piece of poetry in its own right. It is called *Peter Bell the Third*, after Wordsworth's long ballad *Peter Bell*; another parodist had already written *Peter Bell the Second*. Wordsworth's original version is a strange poem, a cross between *The Ancient Mariner* and *The Idiot Boy*; it tells the grotesque story of a wandering good-for-nothing, Peter Bell, whose hard heart is softened by a weird encounter with a dead man and a donkey. Like *The Idiot*

Boy, it is ready-made for easy mockery, but Shelley's poem is far more than a straightforward parody. Shelley sympathized whole-heartedly with Wordsworth's early work and outlook, and what he complains about in his poem is Wordsworth's falling off. He complains that Wordsworth has grown 'dull, beyond all conception dull', and that his verses are now 'the ghosts of what they were', 'Shaking dim gravecloths in the wind'; his early genius has dwindled into 'enormous folly of baptisms, Sunday schools and graves' (a very accurate blow, this, at *The Excursion*); and his thoughts have grown 'weak, drowsy and lame'. This is the indignation of a real admirer, not of an idle scoffer; Shelley is pained by the change. His indignation is at heart political; he is shocked that Wordsworth has deserted the cause of liberty to associate with Tory landowners. The poem contains some malicious remarks about life amongst the footmen at Coleorton, and tea parties in Grosvenor Square. Behind the regret, there is a very real sense of Wordsworth's achievements, and in the following two stanzas he pays a beautiful tribute to the earlier Wordsworth:

> But Peter's verse was clear, and came
> Announcing from the frozen hearth
> Of a cold age, that none might tame
> The soul of that diviner flame
> It augured to the earth:
>
> Like gentle rains on the dry plains
> Making that green which late was grey,
> Or like the sudden moon that stains
> Some gloomy chamber's window panes
> With a broad light like day.

433-42

This is a wonderful description of what Wordsworth did to the barren state of English poetry, at the end of the eighteenth century, that 'frozen hearth of a cold age'; he truly did bring flame and water and light for those who came after him.

Another point which Shelley raises, in passing, is that

Wordsworth's poetry has no sex in it. Shelley calls him 'a solemn and unsexual man' and 'a moral eunuch', and it is quite true that Wordsworth's poetry has very little to do with sex, less perhaps than that of any other great poet except Milton. It would hardly be fair to conclude from this, however, that Wordsworth was not interested in sex; he had, after all, five legitimate children and one illegitimate one, so he must have known something about it. But compared with the highly irregular sex-lives of Shelley, Byron and their circle, his was certainly restrained, and unlike them, he did not put sex into his poetry.

HAZLITT AND BROWNING

Shelley was not the only critic to attack Wordsworth's change of political heart. In later life, he was openly regarded as a turncoat and renegade by some of his old friends: Hazlitt, for instance, wrote a bitter attack on him in 1815 in the *Examiner*, because he had descended to writing 'paltry sonnets' about George the Third. He was attacked in youth for being too revolutionary, and in old age for being reactionary; he suffered both ways, according to the personal politics of his critics. Perhaps the most exaggerated and outspoken attack on his later Tory attitudes was made by Browning in his well-known poem, *The Lost Leader*, which starts off:

> Just for a handful of silver he left us,
> Just for a riband to stick in his coat

—the 'us' presumably meaning high-principled, unmercenary poets like Browning—and which goes on to say:

> Shakespeare was of us, Milton was for us,
> Burns, Shelley were with us—they watch from their graves.
> He alone breaks from the van and the freemen,
> He alone sinks to the rear and the slaves.

These are strong words, and one cannot see that Wordsworth ever did anything bad enough to deserve them; however, this is the price that is often paid by those who change their politics in public.

On the artistic rather than the personal and political side, Wordsworth's first, best and most intelligent critic was undoubtedly his friend Coleridge. From their first meeting until Coleridge's death, they were in close, if not always friendly contact, and they had a powerful effect upon each other. Coleridge's mind was more philosophical and abstract than Wordsworth's, and in later years some of his advice was not as good as it might have been; for instance, it was Coleridge who was so determined that Wordsworth should write 'a great philosophic work' like Milton, and who encouraged him to do so, though his talents did not naturally lead in this direction.

Coleridge wrote at great length about his friend's poetry in his critical work, the *Biographia Literaria*; his chapters on him (14–22) are a reply to and discussion of Wordsworth's own *Preface* to the *Lyrical Ballads*. The *Biographia Literaria* was of course written much later than the *Lyrical Ballads*, and by then the views of both poets had changed. Coleridge is far more subtle and argumentative than Wordsworth; his arguments are too long and complicated to discuss in detail here, but it is worth looking at one or two of the crucial points he raises. One of these is the perennial problem of poetic diction, which Coleridge examines with great penetration. Wordsworth, Coleridge says, asserts that he is using 'the real language of men' in his poems, but this, Coleridge says, is impracticable and useless. No poetry really uses the language of prose; if it did, it would not be poetry. He illustrates his point with the first verse of the *Last of the Flock*:

In distant countries I have been
And yet I have not often seen
A healthy man, a man full grown
Weep in the public roads, alone.

But such a one, on English ground,
And in the broad highway I met;
Along the broad highway he came,
His cheeks with tears were wet:
Sturdy he seemed, though he was sad;
And in his arms a lamb he had.

The actual words here, Coleridge says, are the words of real life, and not of any particular class of society, but they are not in the *order* in which an ordinary person would have put them. A real person, and not a poet, would have told the story more in this way: 'I have been in many parts, far and near, and I don't know that I ever saw before a man crying by himself in the public road; a grown man, I mean . . .'

This is clearly so, and from this Coleridge concludes that the language of poetry cannot possibly be the language of ordinary speech; even if the words are the same, the selection and arrangement of them will be different. The only single example of 'the real and very language of low and rustic life' that he can find in the whole of his friend's work is the last verse of *The Sailor's Mother*.

This is obviously the kind of debate that will never have an ending. What is the real language of men? What men? In what circumstances? Intelligent shepherds, stupid shepherds, emotional shepherds, placid shepherds? And do we include rhyme and metre under the heading of 'language', or just the words themselves? These are the questions that Coleridge goes over, again and again, sorting, defining, re-arranging. There is no final answer, but eventually he comes down more on the side of the poetic than Wordsworth does; he finds Wordsworth at times too mixed in style, at times too matter-of-fact. He prefers, at heart, the lofty Wordsworth, and is offended by sudden changes from the sublime to the everyday. His advice was not always sound; what he did to *The Blind Highland Boy*, for instance, is a wonderful example of mistaken good will.

The poem is a simple ballad about a blind boy who lives by a loch in Scotland, and who one day sets sail on the water and is carried away by the current, quite ignorant of his danger, and to the horror of the villagers, who rush to his rescue. It is a simple, touching poem: a lesser version of *The Idiot Boy*. The dispute arose about the vessel in which the blind boy set sail. In the original story, based on fact, the vessel was a wash-tub; Wordsworth writes:

> But say, what was it? Thought of fear!
> Well may ye tremble when ye hear!
> A household tub, like one of those
> Which women use to wash their clothes,
> This carried the blind boy.

111–15

To Coleridge's more refined imagination, this wash-tub was really too much of a good thing, and he persuaded Wordsworth to change it to a turtle-shell:

> A shell of ample size, and light
> As the pearly car of Amphitrite
> That sportive dolphins drew.

118–20

There are two kinds of Wordsworth readers; those who find the wash-tub ridiculous, and those who find the turtle-shell ridiculous. Nowadays it is more fashionable to find the turtle-shell ridiculous, because it is fanciful, far-fetched, and a most unlikely object to find by a Scottish loch, but naturally enough most people were on Coleridge's side and preferred the shell. It is a question of taste, and every age has its own taste. Doctor Johnson, writing in the eighteenth century, thought Shakespeare showed shocking poetic taste when he wrote the following lines:

> Come, thick night,
> And pall thee in the dunnest smoke of hell,
> That my keen knife see not the wound it makes,
> Nor heaven peep through the blanket of the dark
> To cry 'Hold, hold.'

MACBETH

Words like 'knife', 'blanket' and 'dun', he said, were simply not suitable for serious poetry; they reminded him of butchers, horses and beds. In the same way, wash-tubs reminded Coleridge of washing. Today, poets and critics sympathize more with Shakespeare and Wordsworth than with Johnson and Coleridge; Wordsworth's matter-of-factness, his habit of giving unromantic details of when, who, where and how, is precisely what makes his soldiers and shepherds so much more real and interesting than Gray's and Goldsmith's; it is this that gives them the ring of truth.

MATTHEW ARNOLD AND JOHN STUART MILL

Different ages have different tastes, with the result that people find in a poet what they *want* to find. The Elizabethan Hamlet is a different man from the beautiful velvet-clad Victorian Hamlet, who is different again from the anti-heroic twentieth-century Hamlet with his Oedipus complex. Similarly, the Victorian Wordsworth is a different poet from the Wordsworth of the French Revolution and the *Ballads*. The Victorians found what they were looking for, and they ignored the rest; they looked for flower poetry, for purpureal eves and turtle shells, and they ignored the bath tubs and the idiots. This Victorian Wordsworth is still very much alive today; he is the poet we find in Palgrave's *Golden Treasury*, and the *Oxford Book of English Verse*. This Wordsworth is revealed very clearly by the reactions of two of the most intelligent men of nineteenth-century England: the poet and critic, Matthew Arnold, and the philosopher, John Stuart Mill.

Both these men had a great reverence for Wordsworth, and both found in him the same kind of comfort and inspiration, as their needs were similar. The nineteenth century was a period of acute intellectual doubt; the advance of scientific knowledge, and the over-rapid industrialization of England had between them destroyed much of the traditional way of life, and had shaken men's faith in Christianity. Matthew Arnold was powerfully affected by a sense of his own loss of faith; he was too

K

intelligent to hide his doubts from himself, and yet emotionally he needed to believe. Eventually, instead of seeking comfort in the Church, he came to look for it in literature and the beauties of nature, and Wordsworth was to him a source of great consolation. He acclaimed him as the greatest of the Romantics, and in 1879, thirty years after the poet's death, published a Wordsworth selection, with a critical preface; it was very popular, and caused a mild Wordsworth boom. However, the Wordsworth of his selection is somewhat different from the Wordsworth we admire today. Arnold admires nothing of his earliest work; he is very much a devotee of poems like *The Solitary Reaper* and the *Immortality Ode*. In a poem of praise written after the poet's death, he makes his attitude quite clear; what he admires is 'the soothing voice' and 'healing power' and he says:

> He too upon a wintry clime
> Had fallen—on this iron time
> Of doubts, disputes, distractions, fears,
> He found us when the age had bound
> Our souls in its benumbing round:
> He spoke, and loosed our heart in tears.
> He laid us as we lay at birth,
> On the cool flowery lap of earth. . . .
> Others will strengthen us to bear—
> But who, ah who, will make us feel?
> The cloud of mortal destiny,
> Others will front it fearlessly—
> But who, like him, will put it by?

MEMORIAL VERSES, 42–70

It is easy enough to see from this what Arnold found in Wordsworth; he found an escape from his own 'iron time', with its factory chimneys, railways and disputes about Evolution. He found a tender, beautiful world—the world of the Lake District and the Wordsworth family, cut off, as it certainly was in later years, from the unpleasant struggles of modern life. He found comfort, beauty, refreshment, as an overworked city-worker does on a country holiday. Wordsworth, to Arnold, is a nature-poet and little more. Yet this description of Wordsworth does not fit all the facts, not even all the facts about his attitude to nature. Is 'the cool flowery lap of earth' exactly what he saw in nature? What about the withering celandine, the 'visionary dreariness' of the bleak moors in *The Prelude* and *The Leech Gatherer*, the stormy sea round Peele Castle, the cataracts, the terrors and the admonitions? And does Wordsworth really ignore the fate of mankind, as Arnold suggests? Surely the *Ballads* are full of the most intense sympathy with man, and of a determination to look poverty and old age in the face. One cannot help feeling that Arnold found only what he was looking for, and did not read the rest with much attention; he reads his own doubts and needs into Wordsworth, when they are not always there.

John Stuart Mill was another doubt-ridden Victorian. Like Arnold, he suffered a severe loss of faith, though not of faith in God. He had had a most peculiar upbringing; his father was a great believer in the intellect and in the reformation of society, and he had his son learning Greek by the age of three. It is hard to think of a childhood more different from Wordsworth's own, who at the age of five was not learning Greek, but running in and out of the River Derwent with no clothes on. Mill was a brilliant boy, and appeared to thrive on his forced education, but about the age of twenty-one he had what we would now call a nervous breakdown: he was attacked by fits of deep depression, and lost faith in the ideals on which he had been reared, which now seemed to him dry and hollow. He realized that though he was brilliantly clever, and crammed full of information, he had no heart, no feelings, no pleasure in life, and above all no real understanding of others. In this acute gloom he first came across the poetry of Wordsworth, which was, he says, 'a medicine for my state of mind'. It taught him that life was still worth living; it taught him to feel for ordinary men. In Wordsworth's poems, he says:

I seemed to draw from a source of inward joy, of sympathetic and imaginative pleasure, which could be shared in all human beings . . . from them I seemed to learn what would be the perennial sources of happiness, when the greater evils of life shall have been removed . . . Wordsworth taught me a greatly increased interest in the common feelings and common destiny of human beings.

Wordsworth, one feels, would have been delighted with this tribute, which is in some ways more profound than Arnold's, for it pays attention to Wordsworth's human sympathies, as well as to his love of nature. But both Arnold and Mill agree that Wordsworth is a man of feeling, able to restore warmth of emotion and tenderness to those suffering from a sense of cold emptiness and doubt.

MODERN CRITICS

The idea of Wordsworth as a nature poet, solely and exclusively, has been carried over into our own century from the Victorians, and is still very much alive today. However, there has recently been a revival of enthusiasm for his earliest work. This is not surprising, in view of the nature of modern poetry, much of which is determinedly anti-romantic. Our taste has gone against nature-poetry, and we have started to look for the other Wordsworth. In a book called *The Simple Wordsworth*, for instance, published in 1960, J. F. Danby makes a very strong case for the early ballads; there is an excellent account of *Simon Lee*, which should help to dispel the idea that the poem is no more than a piece of sentimental nonsense about an old man with weak ankles.

There are many modern works on Wordsworth, of varying interest. T. S. Eliot, William Empson, Helen Darbishire and Herbert Read have all made important assessments of him, and Dr. Leavis's essay in his book, *Revaluation*, is particularly well worth attention. Perhaps the most exciting recent full length work is F. W. Bateson's *Wordsworth: A Reinterpretation*, first published in 1954, which interprets Wordsworth's poetry in the

148

light of his life, and which is full of revealing psychological insights. He insists, as Leavis insists, that Wordsworth was not a man of inner tranquility and peace, but a man torn by violent inner conflicts, forever struggling with his own passions, the most disturbing of all being his unnaturally intense affection for his sister Dorothy. He shows most convincingly the way in which Wordsworth's struggles are reflected in his verse.

BIOGRAPHERS

Wordsworth's life story has been interpreted in as many different ways as his poetry. The two most interesting eye-witness accounts could hardly be less similar: one is to be found in Dorothy's *Journal*, the other in de Quincey's *Reminiscences*. Dorothy's *Journal* covers their early years together at Alfoxden and in the Lake District; these were the years of Coleridge and the *Lyrical Ballads*, and of William's marriage to Mary Hutchinson. The *Journal* is full of the homeliest details; Dorothy puts everything down, in a jumble of seriousness and triviality that is life itself, at one moment noting that William is working on his *Ode*, at the next describing the giblet pie she has just made and which was 'not good'. Through the everyday facts it is easy enough to read the deeper preoccupations of her life; her obsessive love for William, her affectionate anxiety about the ill and wretched Coleridge (who seems to have spent much time lying in bed at their cottage persuading Dorothy, instead of his own wife, to provide invalid meals for him), her care of William's children, and her love of nature. Her style is naturally simple, unaffected and readable, and the picture which she draws of the Wordsworth household is one of happy intimacy.

De Quincey's recollections, scattered throughout his works, but gathered together in his *Reminiscences of the English Lake Poets*, could not be more different in tone. He knew the family well, and admired Wordsworth's poetry almost fanatically, but he writes as a journalist. There is nothing artless or unaffected about his style; his attitude is that of a neurotic gossip-columnist. His memories are not at all reverent; he tells us everything:

gossip, anecdotes, descriptions of physical oddities, unfounded bits of scandal, intellectual rhapsodies and mean insinuations are all mixed up together in a strange flow of self-advertisement. His recollections are the kind guaranteed to make the subject's blood run cold, and William was indeed rather dismayed when they were published, although several minor estrangements between the two had already occurred—the source of their first quarrel, we gather, was that the Wordsworth ladies neglected to call on de Quincey's new wife as quickly as they might have done after the marriage. Everything de Quincey says must be taken with a pinch of salt, but the slight edge of malice in his descriptions makes them all the more entertaining, and supplies the other side of Dorothy's perhaps too unqualified praise and love. Both Dorothy and de Quincey write with real immediacy; they show us life in its living detail.

Several full length lives of Wordsworth have appeared since his death. The first of these, by his nephew Christopher, Bishop of Lincoln, is all that might be expected of an admiring and discreet relative: it is solid, respectful and official, and it does not mention Annette Vallon, nor William's sympathy with the now disgraced French Revolution. Professor Knight's biography, published in 1889, is much the same in attitude, and not entirely accurate in its dates. The story of Annette Vallon was first rescued from oblivion by an American scholar, G. M. Harper, and a French critic, Emile Legouis, who between them recovered as many of the facts as were not lost forever. The story can be found in Legouis' *Wordsworth and Annette Vallon* (1922) and in Harper's two-volume *Life* (1916). The latter is an excellent biography, with a very full knowledge of Wordsworth, his poetry, and the historical and intellectual background against which he wrote. There are later and fuller biographies but Harper's remains invaluable, because of his real and sympathetic understanding; he writes from a humanitarian viewpoint very close to Wordsworth's own.

All in all, Wordsworth has been very fully dealt with by wits, journalists, critics and biographers; his position as the greatest poet of the nineteenth century, and as one of the greatest poets of the English language, is not seriously questioned. All that is in doubt is: which Wordsworth is the great one, and which is the one that is better forgotten? There are at least two Wordsworths, as we have seen, and history may produce more. The dispute between the wash-tub admirers and the turtle-shell admirers may rage forever; the wash-tub admirers, triumphant at the moment, may with the turn of taste find themselves deposed once more. As J. K. Stephens wrote, in a parody of Wordsworth's sonnet, *Two voices are there, one is of the sea*:

> Two voices are there; one is of the deep. . . .
> And one is of an old half-witted sheep
> Which bleats articulate monotony. . . .
> And Wordsworth, both are thine.

But which voice is which is still very much a matter of opinion.

Bibliography

STANDARD EDITIONS OF WORDSWORTH'S WORKS

The Poetical Works of William Wordsworth, ed. by E. de Selincourt, 5 vols (Clarendon Press, 1940–49)

The Prelude, ed. by E. de Selincourt, 2nd ed., revised by Helen Darbishire (Clarendon Press, 1959)

SELECTIONS

Wordsworth: *Selected Poetry and Prose*, chosen and edited by John Butt (O.U.P. 1964)

The Poetry of Wordsworth, selected and edited by T. Crehan (University of London Press, 1965.)

NINETEENTH-CENTURY SOURCES

Matthew Arnold: *Essays in Criticism*, 2nd Series (Everyman's Library, 1964)

Matthew Arnold: *Poems*, ed. by Kenneth Allott (Longmans, 1965)

Robert Browning: *The Lost Leader* in *Poems 1833–68* (Oxford Standard Authors)

Lord Byron: *English Bards and Scotch Reviewers* in *Poetical Works* (Oxford Standard Authors)

S. T. Coleridge: *Biographia Literaria* (Everyman's Library, 1956)

Thomas de Quincey: *Reminiscences of the English Lake Poets* (Everyman's Library, 1961)

Thomas de Quincey: *Confessions of an English Opium Eater* (Oxford, World's Classics)

E. de Selincourt (ed.): *The Journals of Dorothy Wordsworth* (Clarendon Press, 1941)

William Hazlitt: *The Spirit of the Age* (Oxford, World's Classics)

Francis Jeffrey: Review of *The Excursion* in the *Edinburgh Review*, Vol. 24, reprinted in *Jeffrey's Literary Criticism*, ed by D. Nichol Smith (Froude, 1910)

W. A. Knight: *Life of W. Wordsworth*, 3 vols (Paterson, 1889)

J. S. Mill: *Autobiography*, Chap. 5 (Oxford, World's Classics)

P. B. Shelley: *Peter Bell the Third* in *Poetical Works* (Oxford Standard Authors)

The Simpliciad (Stockdale, 1808)

Christopher Wordsworth: Memoirs of *William Wordsworth*, 2 vols (Moxon, 1851)

MODERN CRITICISM

E. N. W. Bateson: *Wordsworth. A reinterpretation* (Longmans PB, 1956)

J. F. Danby: *The Simple Wordsworth* (Routledge, 1960)

Helen Darbishire: *The Poet Wordsworth* (Oxford, 1950)

E. de Selincourt: *Dorothy Wordsworth* (Clarendon Press, 1933)

T. S. Eliot: *The Use of Poetry and the Use of Criticism* (Faber PB, 1933)

William Empson: *Seven Types of Ambiguity* (Peregrine PB, 1961)

H. J. C. Grierson: *Milton and Wordsworth* (Cambridge, 1937)

G. M. Harper: *William Wordsworth, his Life, Works and Influence*, 3rd. ed. (Murray, 1927)

F. R. Leavis: *Revaluation*, Chap. 5 (Chatto & Windus, 1953)

Emile Legouis: *William Wordsworth and Annette Vallon* (Dent, 1922)

Emile Legouis: *The Early Life of William Wordsworth*, 2nd ed. (Dent, 1921)

Mary Moorman: *William Wordsworth, the Early Years* (Clarendon Press, 1957)

Mary Moorman: *Wordsworth's Later Years* (Clarendon Press, 1965)

H. D. Rawnsley: *Lake Country Sketches* (MacLehose, 1923)

Sir Herbert Read: *Wordsworth* (Faber, 1949)

General Index

Index to Wordsworth's Poems